Endorsements

"Brian is an expert in the field and ensured we could have these difficult generational conversations in a productive and insightful way. We really appreciate the time and thoughtfulness you put into it."

- California Firefighter Joint Apprenticeship Committee

"Brian has a masterful method of blending intel with practical, relevant business advice. He worked with all generations, from Millennials to Baby Boomers and leaves none in the dark. His business stories were profound, and his entertainment provides the opportunity to absorb strategic points before moving on."

- Global Recruiters Network

"Thank you, Brian, you got all our generations talking and collaborating!"

- The Agape Care Group

"The content Brian provides was invaluable to our group and received high marks on our post conference survey. I'd recommend Brian to anyone seeking a professional and highly engaged speaker."

- International Housewares Association

"Since we got Brian involved, generational differences have been coming up as a topic of conversation in our network in a much more constructive way."

- The New York Small Business Development Council

The Retention Formula: Stop the Turnover Crisis, Harmonize the Generations, and Skyrocket Profits

Published by The Mo Press
Charleston, SC
https://keynotespeakerbrian.com/

ISBN: 979-8-86296-563-6
ISBN: 8-86296-563-6

Library of Congress Cataloging-in-Publication Data
Brian B. Carter
    The Retention Formula: Stop the Turnover Crisis, Lock-In Stability and Skyrocket Profits / Brian B. Carter.
        p. cm.
    Includes bibliographical references and index.
        8-86296-563-6 [979-8-86296-563-6]
    1. Employee Retention I. Generational Differences II. The Retention Formula.

Cover Design by Tracey Kazimir-Cree
Interior Design by Brian Carter

Printed in the United States of America

First Edition: October 8, 2023
10 9 8 7 6 5 4 3 2 1

Table of Contents

Introduction: Welcome to Your Retention Roadmap

Imagine turnover being a distant memory and 95% employee retention your gold standard—does that sound too fantastic?

It needn't be. What's the secret? Generations are not a management headache, but an untapped reservoir of strength.

Why do so many companies struggle with turnover? Often because they're trapped in a one-size-fits-all approach.

This book guides decision-makers to create an environment where people don't just stay but also thrive. We'll delve into your core values, becoming more adaptable, and improving collaboration. I know you probably hear them a lot, but these aren't just buzzwords; they're the pillars of a thriving company.

Contrast that with rigid, hierarchical structures that choke creativity and sap enthusiasm. We'll offer actionable steps, stories, real-world examples, and hypothetical scenarios to bring these principles to life.

With group effort, your organization can reach heights you never anticipated.

So, let's begin this transformative journey together. Are you ready?

Dilemma: Insight into Generational Turnover's Costly Impact

Employee retention is like the sourdough starter of keynote topics—it's super popular though it's featured no more than any other entrée on keynotespeakerbrian.com. When other topics are requested, clients still may say, "Oh, can you also give us a side of employee retention?"

It can seem like young people treat the job market like their Tinder feed—swipe left, swipe left, swipe left, next! Swipe right, two dates, next!

Meanwhile, Boomers and Gen Xers are headed for the exit, not waiting for the retirement cake to cool. Or at least thinking about it. One foot at work and another trying to escape.

So we have many reasons for turnover. And it's expensive. Finding new talent is like upgrading your smartphone every year. Essential? Not sure. Budget-friendly? Definitely not. Turnover doesn't just churn staff; it flushes cash down the drain.

And, shockingly, some out-of-touch leaders still think they can pay newcomers in exposure, retweets, and "resume builders." Sorry, folks, but experience and "good vibes" don't put quinoa bowls on the table—or pay off student loans.

The clash between traditional and modern values is like trying to make a pair of socks out of an old winter hat and a VR headset. That gives us more than just a fashion problem; it produces a culture of misalignment, replacing collaboration with chaos.

Turnover can even be contagious, like a corporate common cold. If the grass seems greener elsewhere, your entire herd may leave. What if Steve from Accounting starts Zoom-chatting with recent ex-coworker Jen, who's now enjoying a pet-friendly office with a bottomless snack bar? Next thing you know, Steve's updating his LinkedIn and applying to share kale chips and casual Fridays with Jen.

This Book: Your One-Stop Shop for Generational Retention Solutions

If you're looking to wind down your HR merry-go-round, you've come to the right place. Consider this your field guide, your operations manual, your "Employee Retention Unleashed"—a title as dynamic as the strategies within.

If you read this book, take its advice to heart, and follow its recommendations, you'll be able to:

- **Decode Youth:** Understand how young people have changed and what that means for you.
- **Navigate Turmoil:** Address the generational issues causing turnover in your organization.
- **Vibe With Z:** Get on the same page with younger people. Learn how to adapt to them, persuade them, and compromise with them.
- **Find the Fit:** Find young people that fit your organization and help them stick.
- **Rocket Fuel Your Culture:** Boost your organization's productivity, morale, and competitiveness.

The bedrock principle is a values-driven approach. Let's get philosophical for a second. Every conflict, every problem, every "Why the heck did they do that?" moment in your organization boils down to just one thing: values. Aligning those values is like tuning an orchestra; get it right, and the music is divine. Get it wrong, you'll be lucky to retain a quartet.

So, you're not just reading a book; you're embarking on a transformative journey. This is your blueprint, your strategy guide—and it comes with a seal of guaranteed effectiveness.

Ready to level up?

Not You: Skip This Book If...

This book is not for everyone. It's tailored for a specific audience, so here's who will most benefit from the insights.

First off, it's designed for those who remember a time before you could put the internet in your pocket, the era of screeching dial-up modems and rotary landlines.

If you're a member of Gen Z or a young Millennial, consider yourself exempt. But if you've noticed older colleagues get confused from things like "BRB," do them a favor—hand them this book. Or keep it if you just want to spy on what we're saying about you! I swear I'll be nice.

Here's who else can skip the checkout:

- **Solo Entrepreneurs:** If you're a one-person show, this might not be a priority. But it could help you work with younger independent contractors.
- **Sales and Marketing Professionals:** While you may glean some ideas, this isn't a comprehensive guide to cracking the Gen Z market.
- **Non-Decision Makers:** If you lack authority, this read may be more frustrating than fruitful. Or read it and pass it on to higher-ups who can enact change.
- **Cost of Business Thinkers:** If what matters to you is that it's more profitable to churn through employees than to fix compensation and culture, this book is not for you.
- **Those Resistant to Change:** Repeating the same actions and expecting different outcomes is a road to nowhere. But if you're not willing to adapt and innovate, you won't unlock the power of this book.
- **Homogeneity Seekers:** If you idealize an office filled with people exactly like you—the same thoughts, looks, and ways of communicating—this book is not your solution. Maybe Mein Kampf is more your speed.
- **Future-Forward Thinkers:** If you're only interested in the work habits of Gen Alpha, first off, they're all well under ten years old, so let's reconvene on this question in a couple of decades.

This book will NOT give you superpowers that change the nature of young people. There are no Jedi mind tricks. However, it does offer effective tools for understanding them and fostering harmony at work.

Finally, this book is not for circus clowns or squirrels, and I'm not allowed to tell you why. They absolutely did not make me say that.

P.S. Send help!

You: The Perfect Audience For this Book

As you might have gathered, this book is for decision-makers – business owners, managers, and executives – age 40 and above who are facing challenges in retaining employees between the ages of 18 and 39. It targets decision-makers who are ready and willing to both see things in a new light and take action to improve their organizations.

A warning: creating change in your organization may also require some internal adjustments on your part. This journey of transformation isn't just about revising company policies or practices; it's also about your own personal growth and adaptability.

Lastly, while this book tackles serious subjects, an open mindset and a good sense of humor will make the process not only enlightening but also enjoyable. After all, effective leadership often includes the ability to take challenges in stride while maintaining a positive outlook.

Advantage: What Makes This Book Unique

Back in 2008, when flared jeans were still a thing and Millennials were just dipping their toes in the professional pool, I dove headfirst into the deep end of managing them.

It started off like a sitcom—complete with misunderstandings and awkward meetings—but soon transformed into a rich learning experience. Fast forward: some of those rookies are still indispensable members of my team. That's in part because I both gained their trust and adapted to them.

Over the past decade, I've earned the title of "Generations Whisperer," advising organizations on how to harmonize interactions across Gen Z, Millennials, Gen X, and Boomers. My experiences span across a wide range of professionals and sectors: from CEOs, CFOs, and marketers to construction workers, cattle feedlot managers, city employees, SaaS salespeople, even military personnel.

My collaborations with esteemed organizations like Pew Research, Deloitte, The Bureau of Labor, and the CIA have provided me with a well-rounded perspective on the complexities of generational dynamics.

That's more than I really want to talk about myself, and part of the reason I start all my keynotes by making fun of my bio.

The theme of this book is consistent: all intergenerational teams face pretty similar challenges. That means the solutions are equally foreseeable. This book is a comprehensive guide to navigating these challenges, building better relationships with younger employees, reducing turnover, and enhancing productivity.

It's not merely a collection of recipes; it's more like a culinary school that teaches skills and tools for creating a harmonious workplace. If you adhere to the principle, your retention soufflé won't fall flat.

So, let's cook up some workplace magic.

Preview: The Sections of the Book

There are six parts of this book, each composed of chapters. Most of the chapters include a variety of content, including research summaries where applicable.

Here's what each section of the book will do for you.

A Story For You

First, tipping my hat to one of my favorite authors and the master of the business fable, Patrick Lencioni, I've crafted a short story that may make it easier for you to get engaged and motivated before making big organizational changes. But if you prefer to get into action quicker, feel free to skip it!

Part I: Diagnosing the Root Cause

Unlock the secrets behind generational turnover to not only identify the key problems but also initiate targeted solutions that save your organization time and money.

Part II: Mapping the Generational Landscape

Get a comprehensive understanding of different generational behaviors, expectations, and strengths. Use this knowledge to adapt your leadership and foster a more harmonious and productive workplace.

Part III: Aligning Corporate and Individual Values

Discover how to align the values of your organization with those of a multigenerational workforce, streamlining your processes and increasing overall efficiency and engagement.

I'll put an asterisk on this part of the book. Although there are many recommendations and action items throughout the book, *I consider the "Rebirth" chapter of Part III the core solution to every problem we discuss. If there's one activity you shouldn't ignore, it's this one.*

Part IV: Actionable Strategies for Retention and Satisfaction

Equip yourself with practical, hands-on strategies to improve communication and teamwork. This part not only addresses problem-solving but also helps you maximize the unique skills each generation brings, optimizing happiness and productivity.

Part V: Leadership and Mentorship

Learn advanced techniques for leading a new, diverse workforce. From knowledge transfer to tailored feedback, this part helps you build a resilient and adaptable team that thrives in any environment.

A Story For You

The Cracks Appear

A Tense Boardroom

It's Monday morning at VirtuFusion, a mid-sized tech company with a staff ranging from Baby Boomers to Gen Z. The mahogany boardroom table is polished to a shine, but the atmosphere is anything but glossy.

Characters

- **Karen:** CEO, a Baby Boomer with a stern demeanor, who's navigated multiple recessions and believes in the tried-and-true
- **Tom:** HR Director, a Gen Xer, caught between adapting to new workplace norms and upholding legacy policies
- **Lisa:** Product Manager, a Millennial with a reputation for innovation but often finds herself hitting the "corporate ceiling"
- **Jack:** Software Engineer, Gen Z, the youngest in the room, often stereotyped as the 'whiz kid' but feeling increasingly disenchanted

Karen settled into her high-back leather chair, cleared her throat, and scanned the room before locking eyes with each board member.

"We've gathered today because we're facing a problem—one that I think we've skirted around for too long," she began. "Our turnover rates have been skyrocketing, and let's be honest, it's mostly our younger talent that's walking out the door."

Tom, with a cup of coffee in hand, looked up from his laptop. "While the numbers do show an uptick, it's not entirely alarming. We're still within industry standards for tech companies our size."

Karen leaned forward. "Tom, we've been 'within industry standards' for so long that it's become a convenient excuse to avoid change. We shouldn't aspire to be average; we should aspire to be exceptional."

Lisa, who had been thumbing through a stack of reports, chimed in. "I can't help but notice that many of the people who've left recently are Millennials or Gen Z. It's a trend we can't ignore."

Tom arched an eyebrow. "Well, isn't that what younger generations do? Job-hop until they find the next best thing?"

Jack, who had been quiet until now, felt a knot tighten in his stomach. He felt seen but not heard, a common feeling that led many of his peers to exit corporate life.

Karen shook her head. "We can stereotype generations all we want, but that's not going to solve the problem. The issue isn't just that they're leaving; it's why they're leaving."

Lisa nodded, "Exactly. We talk about culture and values but when it comes to implementation, we're falling short. We haven't updated our retention strategies in years."

Jack finally decided it was time to speak up. "If I may, there's a general feeling among younger staff that VirtuFusion is kind of stuck in the past. The 'antiwork' sentiment is real, and it's not just about being lazy or entitled. It's about wanting work to be more than just a paycheck."

The room went silent for a moment. Each one was contemplating Jack's words, realizing the weight they carried.

Karen sighed, "If we're going to point fingers, let's make sure we're also pointing them at ourselves. This isn't a Gen Z problem, a Millennial problem, a Gen X problem, or a Boomer problem. This is a VirtuFusion problem."

Tom set his coffee down. "So, what's the plan?"

Karen looked at each of them, realizing that the path ahead was uncertain but necessary.

"The plan is to stop planning within the confines of what's comfortable. We need to dig deep, challenge our preconceptions, and actually listen to our employees—regardless of when they were born. We're going to delve into this, and we're going to do it as one team."

Each person in the room nodded, silently acknowledging the complex journey ahead. It was a collective realization that they were in uncharted waters, requiring more than just a compass of past experiences. They needed a new map, one that included all the generational landmarks.

The Shocking News

The atmosphere in the VirtuFusion boardroom is still tense, but now tinged with a sense of urgency. It's only been fifteen minutes since the meeting started, but it feels much longer.

Karen shifted in her chair and glanced at a closed folder in front of her. She took a deep breath before opening it and pulling out a single sheet of paper.

"I have another matter that I believe will underscore the urgency of what we're dealing with," she said, her voice faltering for just a moment. "Sarah, our rising star in data analytics, has tendered her resignation."

Tom's eyes widened, and he put down his cup of coffee so abruptly it nearly spilled. "Sarah? She was on track for a leadership role. What happened?"

"According to her resignation letter, she's received an offer from a competitor. And before you ask, yes, we did make a counteroffer. She declined," Karen explained, her face a mask of controlled concern.

Lisa and Jack exchanged a quick glance. Neither of them looked surprised.

"Ah, so she's chasing a fatter paycheck," Tom muttered, almost to himself.

Lisa shook her head. "It's not always about money, Tom. Some of us want more than just a well-stocked 401(k). We want to feel like we're part of something bigger. And sometimes, we need to see proof that the company is willing to change for the better."

Jack felt a sense of validation hearing Lisa's words. "Sarah was one of the most vocal advocates for change in how we manage projects and teams. She felt stifled here, and many of us feel the same way."

Tom looked from Lisa to Jack, his face reflecting a mix of skepticism and begrudging acceptance. "So, you're saying she left because we're...what? Not progressive enough?"

Karen leaned back, absorbing the dynamics playing out in front of her. "She left because she didn't see a future here that aligned with her values. And that's something we all need to think about."

Silence enveloped the room. Each person there, representing different generations and perspectives, had to confront the reality that Sarah's exit was a symptom of a much bigger issue. An issue that wouldn't just resolve itself with time or even money.

As they sat in thoughtful quietude, they each began to appreciate the magnitude of the task that lay ahead: transforming a workplace culture deeply entrenched in old norms into one that could bridge generational divides.

Karen broke the silence. "Let's move on to the next agenda item. But I want you all to think hard about what's just been discussed. The change we need won't happen overnight, but it needs to start today."

The team members nodded, their minds already buzzing with ideas, challenges, and the stark realization that the road ahead was going to be a bumpy ride.

The Uncomfortable Reality

A quiet tension settles over the VirtuFusion boardroom. The team has moved through other agenda items but keeps circling back to the topic of turnover. The late afternoon sun casts long shadows on the table.

Karen reached for the remote control and dimmed the display screen at the front of the room.

"Alright, we've discussed metrics, we've looked at our competitors, and we've reviewed our existing policies. Let's not dance around the issue anymore. What's really going on here? Why are we failing to retain our younger employees?"

Tom, who had been taking meticulous notes, sighed. "Maybe it's the industry. Everyone's saying tech has a revolving door."

Lisa raised an eyebrow. "So, you're suggesting this is a systemic problem we can't do anything about?"

Tom shook his head, "No, not exactly. I'm saying it might be bigger than us. But it doesn't mean we can't be better than most."

Jack decided to jump in. "We can definitely be better. We're not a startup, but we're not a behemoth either. We have the flexibility to change—if we want to."

Karen nodded, visibly pleased. "I agree with Jack. We have the ability to change, but we need to be willing to make uncomfortable choices. So, what are we missing? What do our employees need that we're not providing?"

The room fell silent for a moment as each person contemplated the question.

Finally, Lisa spoke, "I think we're missing empathy. We're not putting ourselves in their shoes. We have policies designed for a workforce that no longer exists in the same way."

Tom looked skeptical but intrigued. "Empathy, you say?"

"Yes," Lisa continued, "empathy in understanding what they value—flexibility, personal development, a voice in decision-making, and social responsibility. Empathy in how we communicate those values and actually implement them."

Jack chimed in, "And it's not just policies. It's also about day-to-day interactions, immediate feedback, and having a sense of community, even in a remote work setting."

Karen absorbed their insights and finally spoke, "So, to summarize, we need to modernize not just our policies but also our attitudes. Empathy, flexibility, and community should be our new guideposts."

Each nodded, sensing that they had reached a tipping point. Tom was the first to break the silence, "It's going to be a huge shift. How do we even start?"

Karen smiled, a glimmer of hope in her eyes. "We start by acknowledging that we don't have all the answers, but we have the will to find them. And that process begins with listening—truly listening—to what our employees have to say."

And with that acknowledgment, the members of the VirtuFusion executive team realized they were stepping into a new era, an era defined not by generational divides but by a shared vision of what a truly inclusive, empathetic, and forward-thinking workplace could look like.

Facing The Hard Truths

The Town Hall

A spacious conference hall at the VirtuFusion headquarters, converted into a town hall meeting space. Employees from different departments and generations are seated, chatting amongst themselves with curious expressions. A podium stands at the front, next to a large projector screen.

Characters

- **Karen:** The Baby Boomer CEO, anxious but committed to opening a dialogue
- **Tom:** Gen X HR Director, cautiously optimistic
- **Lisa:** Millennial Product Manager, hopeful that real change could be on the horizon
- **Jack:** Gen Z Software Engineer, attending his first-ever corporate town hall

Karen looked over her notes one last time before stepping up to the podium. The chatter in the room subdued as she tapped the microphone.

"Good afternoon, everyone. Thank you for being here. Today we're doing something different—a town hall to discuss a topic that affects us all: employee retention and workplace culture."

Murmurs spread across the room. People exchanged glances; the issue had been a subject of watercooler talks for months.

Tom stood to the side, eyeing the crowd, trying to gauge their reactions. Lisa and Jack were seated among their peers, tensely optimistic.

"Our aim is not to come up with quick fixes but to listen and understand what we, as a company, can do better," Karen continued, clearly trying to set the stage for an open discussion.

She opened the floor to questions and comments. At first, silence. Then, a hand went up. A young data analyst spoke about the need for mentorship programs tailored for younger employees.

Another hand. A middle-aged project manager talked about how an inflexible work schedule affected his ability to spend time with his family.

Tom scribbled notes furiously, realizing that some concerns transcended generational boundaries.

Jack felt a surge of courage and raised his hand. Karen acknowledged him, "Yes, Jack?"

"Um, hi. I haven't been here long, but I've noticed that there's not much space for innovation or risk-taking. Everything feels set in stone, and it's discouraging for those of us who want to bring fresh ideas to the table."

Karen nodded, "Thank you, Jack. That's an invaluable insight."

As the session progressed, Lisa felt increasingly validated. The discussions highlighted that employees of all ages were facing issues that stemmed from an outdated workplace culture. She met Tom's eyes across the room, and for the first time, they shared a nod of agreement. Maybe they were finally getting somewhere.

Karen closed the meeting by thanking everyone for their honesty. "Your voices have been heard, and we're committed to initiating change. We'll be setting up working groups to dig into these issues in detail, and I encourage each of you to participate."

As people filed out of the conference hall, there was a palpable sense of cautious optimism. The journey was far from over, but the first steps had been taken.

Karen, Tom, Lisa, and Jack gathered for a brief moment at the front of the room. Each felt the weight of the challenges ahead but also a newfound sense of unity and purpose.

"We've got a lot of work to do," Karen said, looking at each of them in turn.

They all agreed, in different words and almost in unison. But for the first time, they all believed that the work was not just necessary but possible.

Working Groups

Several small meeting rooms at VirtuFusion, each hosting a different working group. The atmosphere is a mix of skepticism and cautious optimism. Whiteboards are filled with ideas and post-its.

Karen stepped into the first meeting room, where Tom was leading a discussion on flexibility and work-life balance. She listened as a diverse group of employees passionately discussed the pros and cons of flexible work schedules, remote work, and job-sharing.

"I think we can pilot a 4-day workweek in departments where it makes sense," Tom suggested, and the room erupted into both supportive and skeptical voices.

Across the hall, Lisa's working group was buzzing with energy. Employees from all generations discussed how the company could foster a culture of innovation and risk-taking.

"What if we allocate 10% of work hours to personal projects or cross-departmental collaborations?" Lisa offered.

"I like the idea, but how would we measure success or ROI?" questioned an older marketing executive.

Jack, who was part of the group, spoke up, "Maybe it's not just about immediate ROI. It could lead to more engaged employees, better inter-departmental understanding, and in the long term, unexpected but valuable innovations."

Karen, who had just entered the room, caught Jack's comment and smiled. The young software engineer was holding his own among more experienced colleagues.

As the working groups wrapped up, each team had a list of actionable items, timelines, and volunteers who would lead each initiative. Karen gathered Tom, Lisa, and Jack for a quick debrief.

"So, what do you think? Was it a productive day?" Karen asked.

Tom was the first to speak, "I think we're heading in the right direction. There's enthusiasm, but also a lot of questions and concerns. It's going to be a balancing act."

Lisa added, "I agree. There's a willingness to try new things, but we also have to be careful not to alienate those who are comfortable with the status quo."

Jack finally spoke, "For what it's worth, today made me feel hopeful. It's the first time I've seen people from different parts of the company and different generations come together to solve problems."

Karen looked at each of them, seeing the beginning of a transformational team. "Well, we've planted the seeds. Let's commit to nurturing them and see what grows."

As they left the meeting rooms, each was aware of the monumental task ahead. But for the first time, they also felt an invigorating sense of possibility and collective will.

The Executive Briefing

A sleek boardroom at VirtuFusion headquarters. A large table dominates the room, surrounded by leather chairs. A projector is ready for presentations. The atmosphere is one of anticipation mixed with skepticism.

As Karen welcomed everyone to the meeting, Tom shuffled his notes, Lisa rehearsed her key points in her mind, and Jack fidgeted with a pen, his usual fidget spinner left back at his desk for the sake of professionalism.

Tom was the first to present. He laid out a comprehensive proposal for introducing flexible work arrangements, complete with pilot programs, KPIs, and contingency plans. As he answered questions from the executive team, he felt their skepticism but also a surprising openness to trying something new.

Next up was Lisa, who unveiled her group's plan to foster innovation and risk-taking. She explained the idea of "Innovation Time Off" and how it could be measured qualitatively rather than just through immediate ROI.

The executive team grilled Lisa with questions, but she remained steadfast, her answers well-reasoned and supported by data. Karen was impressed, not just by the proposals but by Lisa's growth into a confident, persuasive leader.

Finally, Karen turned to Jack, "We've invited Jack to offer a Gen Z perspective on the proposed changes. Jack?"

Jack rose, his legs a little shaky. "From what I've seen, these proposals aren't just about fixing a broken system. They're about creating a new one, where everyone, from Baby Boomers to Gen Z, can contribute and feel valued."

The room was silent, then Karen broke the silence. "Thank you, Jack. That's exactly the point we're aiming for."

The executive team began discussing the proposals in earnest. Each had reservations, but there was a sense that change was not only necessary but possible and even exciting. Karen felt a weight lift off her shoulders. The executive team was behind her, and more importantly, behind the need for change.

After the meeting adjourned, Karen, Tom, Lisa, and Jack gathered outside the boardroom.

"Whatever happens next, today was a win," Karen said.

Tom nodded, "Agreed. And we couldn't have done it without the insights and hard work from every generation in this company."

Lisa chimed in, "It feels like we're on the cusp of something big."

Jack grinned, "Yeah, something that could make VirtuFusion a place where people not only want to work but want to stay."

Karen looked at her diverse, multi-generational team. "Alright, let's take this momentum and run with it. The real work starts now."

As they dispersed, each felt a sense of accomplishment but also an acute awareness that the journey was far from over. Yet, for the first time, the path ahead seemed not just challenging but also profoundly rewarding.

Turning the Ship

Pilot Programs Begin

Various locations within VirtuFusion, from office cubicles to communal working spaces. Employees are navigating the new changes, with mixed feelings and varying levels of success.

Characters

- **Karen:** The Baby Boomer CEO, watching carefully as the pilot programs roll out, eager for them to succeed but aware that there might be pitfalls.
- **Tom:** Gen X HR Director, managing the Flexible Work Arrangements program and juggling between different issues.
- **Lisa:** Millennial Product Manager, shepherding the Innovation Time Off initiative, excited but a bit anxious.
- **Jack:** Gen Z Software Engineer, participating in the Innovation Time Off, collaborating on a new project.

Karen roamed the office, keenly observing employees as they adjusted to the new policies. She noticed a few older employees struggling to adapt to the flexible schedules, while younger employees seemed more at ease.

Meanwhile, Tom found himself fielding questions left and right, from "How does the 4-day workweek affect my vacation days?" to "How do we manage client expectations with these new hours?"

Tom was tired but determined. "We're ironing out the kinks. It's a pilot, after all. We'll adapt as we go."

Across the floor, Lisa was buzzing with energy as she went from one team to another, encouraging employees to pitch their innovative ideas. Some were enthusiastic, but others were skeptical, wondering whether the company would really invest in them.

"Remember, this is not just an experiment," she told her team. "It's a commitment from the top to nurture a culture of innovation."

Jack was in a meeting room with a whiteboard, brainstorming with a small team as part of the Innovation Time Off. They were developing a new tool that would automate part of their workflow. Despite a few technical challenges, the project showed promise, and Jack felt invigorated.

However, not everyone was pleased. Some employees felt that the new changes disrupted their work routine and added complexity to their day-to-day tasks.

Karen, aware of the murmurs of discontent, decided it was time for another company-wide meeting. She arranged for a town hall to be held at the end of the week to address questions and concerns.

As the characters regrouped at the end of the day, there was a sense of cautious optimism but also an undercurrent of stress and uncertainty.

Karen met briefly with Tom, Lisa, and Jack. "So, day one of the new world. How did we fare?"

Tom sighed, "Mixed reviews, but that's to be expected."

Lisa was upbeat, "We've seen some really interesting project proposals already."

Jack added, "Yeah, there's excitement but also confusion. Clear communication will be key moving forward."

Karen nodded. "Alright, let's keep the dialogue open. We'll address concerns in the town hall and keep refining our approach. This is a marathon, not a sprint."

As they left for the day, each knew that the road ahead was long and fraught with challenges. However, the shared belief that they were moving toward a more inclusive, effective, and vibrant work environment kept their spirits high.

Second Town Hall

The company's large auditorium, filled with employees from all departments and all age groups. A stage is set up at the front with chairs and microphones for the speakers. A large screen displays the VirtuFusion logo.

Karen stepped onto the stage, taking the microphone with a shaky hand but a strong voice. "Thank you all for coming today. As you know, we're in the early stages of several pilot programs aimed at making VirtuFusion a better place to work for everyone, regardless of generation. Today is about hearing from you."

Tom was next, sharing preliminary data on the new flexible work arrangements. He explained how the 4-day workweek was affecting productivity, work-life balance, and overall job satisfaction. The numbers were promising but not conclusive.

Lisa followed, excitedly sharing two projects that had already emerged from the Innovation Time Off. "These are the kinds of game-changing ideas that can happen when we give ourselves the time and space to think creatively," she declared.

Then came time for Q&A. Hands shot up, and a variety of questions and comments filled the room.

A Baby Boomer in Sales questioned, "I understand the need for flexibility, but some of us have client obligations that can't be confined to a 4-day workweek."

A Millennial from Marketing added, "I love the innovation time, but it's hard to focus on it when we're still expected to meet all our regular deadlines."

Jack took the stage as part of an employee panel. He acknowledged that not all the changes were perfect but emphasized that they were a step in the right direction. "We're building something new here, something that respects the needs and talents of every generation. That's going to take time and effort from all of us."

Karen closed the meeting, "We've heard you, and we're committed to fine-tuning these programs to make them as effective as possible. But we can't do it without your continued feedback and engagement. Let's continue to build a VirtuFusion where every voice is heard, and every generation can thrive."

As the room emptied, Karen, Tom, Lisa, and Jack met backstage. Each was a mix of relief and renewed determination.

Tom sighed, "Well, that could have gone worse."

Lisa added, "And it could have gone better. But it's a start."

Jack was optimistic, "The key takeaway for me is that people care. They wouldn't speak up if they didn't."

Karen looked at her team, "Alright, let's regroup early next week to discuss adjustments based on today's feedback. The journey continues."

As they left the auditorium, they felt the weight of their responsibilities but also a growing confidence that they were on the path to creating a work environment that could truly bridge generational divides.

Adjustments and Alliances

A conference room within VirtuFusion, the walls adorned with charts and plans. The table is covered with laptops, documents, and cups of coffee. It's a war room atmosphere, where strategy is being finalized.

As the team sat down, Karen cleared her throat, "Okay, folks, we've gotten some valuable feedback, both positive and negative. Now it's time to adjust. Where do we start?"

Tom had a spreadsheet open, "The 4-day workweek is well-received overall, but there are valid concerns from client-facing roles. We might need to introduce a rotation system."

Lisa interjected, "On the Innovation Time Off front, it seems like people are overwhelmed. Maybe we can consider a phased approach, rolling it out to one department at a time?"

Jack nodded, "I also think we should keep emphasizing training on the new technologies. The older workforce seems reluctant because they're unfamiliar with the tools."

Karen was pleased with the suggestions. "Excellent points, all around. Tom, can you revise the flexible schedule program to address the client-facing roles? And Lisa, let's try a phased approach with Innovation Time Off."

Tom agreed, "Certainly, I'll draft a new outline by the end of the day."

Lisa chimed in, "I can identify a department where we can test the phased approach. How about we try it with the Marketing team?"

"Sounds good," Karen approved. "And Jack, can you work with HR to set up some basic tech tutorials? Let's make sure everyone feels comfortable with the new systems."

"Absolutely," Jack replied, "I know some folks in IT who'd be great for leading those sessions."

As the meeting came to a close, Karen looked at her team, feeling a mix of exhaustion and optimism. "We're making progress, folks. We've listened, we've learned, and now we adjust. Keep your ears to the ground and be ready to adapt further. We're writing a new chapter for VirtuFusion, and it requires our best efforts."

With that, they went their separate ways, eager to implement the changes. The atmosphere was tense but hopeful. They knew that the road ahead was filled with challenges but also ripe with opportunities for transformative success.

Bridging The Divide

New Horizons

Various locations within VirtuFusion, transitioning from department to department. The scene takes the viewer through a series of vignettes that show the programs in action after the adjustments made in Act III.

Characters
- **Karen:** The Baby Boomer CEO, visible through company-wide announcements and seen informally checking in on different departments.
- **Tom:** Gen X HR Director, facilitating training sessions and seen handing out new policy documents.
- **Lisa:** Millennial Product Manager, leading an innovation brainstorm session with the Marketing team.
- **Jack:** Gen Z Software Engineer, co-hosting a tech tutorial.
- **Employees:** Interacting with the main characters, some skeptical, some hopeful, but all more engaged than before.

Karen stood before a camera, recording a company-wide announcement. "Hello, VirtuFusion team. We heard you at the town hall, and we've made some adjustments to our pilot programs. I hope you'll find these changes responsive to your concerns."

Simultaneously, Tom was seen facilitating a workshop on the new, flexible rotation system for client-facing roles. A Baby Boomer employee raised her hand, "This is a much better compromise. I can now balance my client meetings without feeling rushed."

Cut to Lisa, in a conference room with the Marketing team, a whiteboard filled with ideas. "Okay, folks, we're the first department to test the phased Innovation Time Off. Let's make it count!" A Millennial team member chimed in, "I've been waiting for an opportunity to work on some of these side projects. This is great!"

Next, Jack was seen in a computer lab, co-hosting a tech tutorial. A Gen X employee approached him afterward, "I have to admit, I was skeptical, but seeing how these tools can make my job easier is eye-opening."

As the day progressed, Karen walked through the hallways, popping into different departments. She stopped to chat with employees, asking about their experiences with the new changes. The responses varied but were generally positive.

Back in her office, Karen felt cautiously optimistic. She knew there would still be bumps in the road, but the general atmosphere had shifted from skepticism to constructive engagement.

Her phone buzzed; it was a message from Tom: "Initial feedback on rotations is positive. Details in your email."

Then a notification from Lisa: "First innovation session was a hit. Lots of energy and ideas."

Finally, a text from Jack: "Tech tutorial went well. Already have requests for more sessions."

Karen leaned back in her chair and took a deep breath. For the first time in months, she felt not just hopeful, but confident. VirtuFusion was truly beginning to change, and she couldn't wait to see where this new chapter would lead.

The Trial by Fire

A crisis management meeting room at VirtuFusion, filled with palpable tension. Screens display real-time data, showing some fluctuations in team productivity and employee satisfaction.

Karen called the meeting to order, "Alright, team, I've seen the reports, and we've hit some bumps. What's going on?"

Tom was the first to speak, gesturing towards a graph on the screen, "We've had some pushback on the rotation system. A few key clients have expressed concern about the changing points of contact. We need to address this quickly."

Lisa looked worried, "On my end, the Innovation Time Off is generating good ideas but disrupting regular workflows. Deadlines are getting missed."

Jack chimed in, "And the tech tutorials, while helpful for some, have also created a bit of an 'us-versus-them' mentality. I've heard comments that they make some long-term employees feel 'obsolete'."

Karen took a deep breath, "Okay, these are real issues, but they're also growing pains. They give us valuable insights into where we need to adjust further."

Tom suggested, "For the rotation system, we could assign client-relations specialists who maintain consistency in client communications while the primary contacts rotate."

Lisa thought for a moment, "Maybe we can integrate Innovation Time Off with ongoing projects, so it complements rather than disrupts regular work."

Jack added, "As for the tech tutorials, perhaps we can frame them as 'skill-sharpening sessions' for everyone, not just those unfamiliar with the technology."

Karen nodded, "Excellent ideas, all. Let's put these into action immediately and monitor the impact. We knew this wasn't going to be easy, but we're committed to making it work. Keep the lines of communication open, and be ready to adapt, yet again."

As they adjourned, each member felt a combination of concern and renewed determination. They were reminded that change is hard, messy, and fraught with challenges, but they were united in their mission to steer VirtuFusion through these turbulent waters.

The Turning Tide

Various locations around VirtuFusion—each character is seen in their respective domain, going about their duties. The atmosphere is lighter than in the previous scenes, with snippets of positive conversations heard in passing.

Karen was in her office, scanning through the most recent reports. For the first time in months, the numbers were encouraging. Employee satisfaction had seen a significant uptick, and turnover rates were down. A soft knock on the door interrupted her concentration. It was Tom, walking in with a tablet in hand.

"Karen, you'll want to see this," he said, handing her the device with a dashboard displaying upward trends in key performance metrics. "We've been monitoring since the new initiatives were rolled out. It's still early, but we're moving in the right direction."

Karen looked at the tablet, her eyes widening as she scanned the graphs. "This is impressive, Tom. Really impressive. But let's not get ahead of ourselves; we've still got work to do."

Cut to Lisa, who was celebrating a project milestone with her team in a conference room. A small cake sat in the center of the table, alongside a few bottles of sparkling cider. She stood up and raised a glass. "Great job, everyone! Our recent success proves that Innovation Time Off isn't just a 'feel-good' policy; it's essential for our growth."

Her team clinked glasses, and their faces lit up with genuine smiles. "To more innovation and less burnout!" someone yelled, and the room erupted in laughter and agreement.

Meanwhile, Jack was at his desk in a sea of cubicles, diligently typing away at his keyboard. A message popped up on his computer screen: "Hey, thanks for the tutorial last week, really cleared things up for me. When's the next one?"

A smile crossed his face as he read the message. He was quick to draft a response. "Glad you found it useful! Next session is on Friday. We'll be diving into API integrations. See you there!"

Back in Karen's office, she hosted a virtual meeting with Tom, Lisa, and Jack. The atmosphere was different this time—less tense, more collaborative. "We've made some excellent progress, and for that, I want to say thank you. But let's remember, this is just the beginning. Change is an ongoing process, and we'll need to be agile."

Lisa nodded, her image framed by the backdrop of her living room. "Absolutely, Karen. This is a marathon, not a sprint. And there's still a long road ahead."

Jack chimed in, the youthful energy in his voice adding a dose of optimism to the conversation. "Right, we keep refining as we go. Taking feedback, making adjustments, and moving forward."

Karen felt a sense of pride wash over her. She had steered her company through one of its toughest phases, and while the path ahead was still uncertain, the journey itself had united them. "Thank you all for your dedication, your resilience, and your willingness to adapt. We've set a new course for VirtuFusion, and while the seas ahead may still be choppy, I couldn't have asked for a better crew to navigate them with."

The screen faded to black, signaling the end of the act, but not the end of the journey for VirtuFusion or its dedicated team.

A New Dawn

The New Horizon

VirtuFusion's office atrium. A sense of occasion fills the air. A podium stands near a banner that reads: "VirtuFusion: Navigating the Future, Together."

Characters
- **Karen:** The Baby Boomer CEO, standing near the podium with a speech in hand.
- **Tom:** Gen X HR Director, mingling with employees, smiling.
- **Lisa:** Millennial Product Manager, looking excited and nervous.
- **Jack:** Gen Z Software Engineer, immersed in conversation with a group of diverse employees.
- **Employees:** In higher spirits than before, visibly excited about the event.

Karen stood beside the podium, scanning the crowd of expectant faces. She could feel the weight of the moment, not just for her but for every employee under the banner of VirtuFusion. She took a deep breath and stepped up to the microphone.

"Good afternoon, everyone," Karen began, her voice resonating throughout the atrium. "We're gathered here today not just to celebrate our recent successes but to lay the cornerstone for the future of VirtuFusion."

The crowd erupted in applause, an undeniable sign of newfound unity and common purpose.

Tom was speaking with a group of employees about upcoming skill-building workshops. He was no longer seen as a harbinger of bad news but as a gatekeeper to opportunities for growth. "Think of these as your toolkit for navigating the future," he told them, handing out flyers that listed the upcoming workshops.

Lisa stood next to a poster board displaying VirtuFusion's latest product launch. "And this," she pointed to a graph showing positive user feedback, "is why your Innovation Time Off is so vital. You've given us fresh perspectives and look where it got us!"

Her team members nodded, visibly pleased and eager to contribute more.

Meanwhile, Jack was engrossed in a discussion about the future of technology at VirtuFusion. "Our next step is integrating artificial intelligence to automate some of the mundane tasks. Think of what we can do with that extra time for creative work!"

Karen returned to the microphone as the atmosphere reached a palpable sense of enthusiasm. "Before we wrap up, I want to share something personal," she paused, looking at her team with sincere gratitude. "Months ago, we were on the brink. Today, we're standing at the threshold of a new era. This transformation didn't happen by accident. It happened because each one of you chose to engage, to change, to fight for this company's future."

The crowd stood in applause, tears of relief and joy mingling in more than a few eyes.

She continued, "We've been like a ship sailing through a storm, battered yet unbroken. But remember, the key to reaching calm waters wasn't just in surviving the storm; it was in learning how to navigate through it. Together."

As Karen concluded, the room erupted in cheers, claps, and even a few hugs. While the future was still uncertain, one thing was clear: VirtuFusion had found its North Star, and they would follow it, no matter what lay ahead.

The Power of Shared Success

VirtuFusion's modernized workspace. Sunlight filters through large windows, casting a warm glow on the various workstations, open spaces, and conference rooms. It's an ordinary workday, but there's a palpable sense of purpose in the air.

As Karen pored over the quarterly reports on her screen, a smile crept onto her face. Sales were up, and retention rates had improved significantly. She saved the document and stood up, deciding to take a walk around the office.

Tom was holding a workshop on "Leadership Across Generations." A mix of young and old faces listened intently, notebooks and laptops ready to capture his insights. "Remember, great leadership isn't confined to an age bracket or a management title. It's about understanding the intrinsic values that drive people, and channeling that energy towards shared goals."

A nod of acknowledgment swept across the room. VirtuFusion had become a place where expertise was valued, but so was the willingness to learn and adapt.

In another corner of the office, Lisa was showing her team the ropes of a new project management software. "This will streamline our workflow and keep everyone in the loop. No more endless email threads, okay?"

Her team chuckled. The atmosphere was relaxed, yet everyone knew the importance of what they were doing. They respected Lisa not just for her managerial skills but for her ability to relate to each one of them.

Meanwhile, Jack was immersed in building a prototype for a new feature that had been suggested during the last team meeting. He toggled between coding and a design interface, clearly in his element. He paused to send a quick message on the company chat: "Hey team, could use some input on this. Anyone free for a quick brainstorm?"

Within seconds, two colleagues from different departments responded. A few minutes later, they were gathered around Jack's desk, engaged in a lively discussion.

Karen arrived back at her office, inspired by what she had seen. She felt confident that the culture at VirtuFusion had not only turned a corner but was accelerating down a new, more promising path.

Just as she was about to sit back down, her assistant knocked on the door. "Karen, a moment?"

"Of course, come in."

"I just wanted to hand-deliver this," her assistant said, passing her a thank-you card signed by several employees. "It's from the team that went through the mentorship program. They wanted you to know how much they appreciated the opportunity."

Karen opened the card and read the heartfelt messages. Tears welled up in her eyes. This, she thought, is what true leadership feels like. It wasn't just about profits or productivity; it was about creating a space where everyone felt valued, a place where each generation could contribute to a legacy of shared success.

And so, under the unassuming rays of an ordinary afternoon sun, the people of VirtuFusion found themselves bound by a newfound purpose, each contributing a verse to an unfolding narrative of redemption, growth, and unity.

The Circle of Trust and Triumph

VirtuFusion's conference room, transformed into an awards ceremony space for the day. Employees of all ages gather around, chatter filling the room as excitement builds for the company's inaugural "Unity Awards."

As Karen stood at the podium, she felt the collective energy of a team that had come together across generational lines. She tapped the microphone, and the room fell silent.

"Welcome to the first annual Unity Awards. Before we begin, I want to say that this isn't just about recognizing a few individuals; it's about celebrating what we've built together as a community."

Nods and claps filled the room. Tom, who had now moved closer to the podium, exchanged an approving look with Karen.

"The first award is for 'Best Cross-Generational Collaboration.' And this goes to Lisa and Jack for their project on integrating AI into our customer service system!"

Lisa and Jack walked up to the podium amidst applause, their faces glowing with pride and surprise. After accepting the award, they returned to their seats, barely containing their excitement.

Karen continued, "The next award is for 'Lifetime Mentorship.' This goes to someone who has been an anchor in bridging generational gaps—Tom."

Tom walked up to the podium, his eyes moist. Karen handed him a plaque, which he held as if it were a treasured heirloom.

"Thank you, Karen, thank you, team. This is more than an award; it's proof that when we unite, we become a force greater than the sum of our individual efforts."

The ceremony continued, with various awards recognizing talents, efforts, and most importantly, unity among the diverse group.

After the ceremony, Karen returned to her office, the plaques now distributed, the room empty but for the echoes of a newfound camaraderie.

Sitting at her desk, she looked at a framed picture of the company's first-ever team—a much smaller group, but a poignant reminder of where they had started. Then, she opened her drawer and took out the Unity Awards' master list, placing it next to the photo.

As she sat there, savoring the moment, her phone buzzed. It was a message from the Board of Directors. The text read, "Congratulations on the successful quarter and the Unity Awards. You've turned this ship around."

Karen smiled, her eyes lingering on the old photo and then on the new list. The ship hadn't just turned around; it had found its North Star, in a sky brightened by the constellation of multiple generations.

For Karen, and for VirtuFusion, this wasn't an end, but a hopeful beginning, one that promised the treasures of trust, unity, and success in many years to come.

And thus, the curtain closes on our tale of generational unity at VirtuFusion. Yet, in the silence that follows the applause, a message reverberates—unity isn't a final destination but an ongoing journey, one that enriches both the travelers and the world they traverse.

Part I: Diagnosing the Root Cause

The core causes of turnover are:

- People and cultures change.
- People resist change.
- Organizations end up with a hodgepodge of mismatched values, injuring culture, teamwork, and satisfaction.

We'll solve those problems together by:

- **Decoding** trends so you can manage them,
- **Understanding** the power of adaptability so that you can improve your organization, and
- **Building** common ground to increase your influence, build teamwork and boost retention.

Leaks: Why Generational Turnover is Costing You Money and How to Stop It

1. Rebellion: How to Prevent an 'Antiwork' Mass Exodus

Do you realize something fundamental is shifting in how people think about work? The signs are out there — flickering on our screens, animating late-night discussions, and fueling debates that are no longer relegated to ivory towers but have spilled into the streets of everyday life.

Welcome to the era of 'Antiwork,' a term that is as misunderstood as it is transformative.

Imagine Alex, scrolling through Reddit on his smartphone after a grueling 12-hour workday. He stumbles across the *r/antiwork* subreddit — a burgeoning digital community that, as of 2023, boasts 2.8 million members, with at least 22,000 people actively engaged at any given time.

In this online space, Alex finds a chorus of voices that echo his own frustrations. It's like he's walked into a room full of strangers and discovered they're all singing his favorite song.

The term "antiwork" may evoke thoughts of laziness or lack of ambition, but the reality is much more nuanced.

It's not about refusing to work, but refusing to accept:

- **Overwork:** The chronic fatigue that erodes mental and physical health, leaving people as burnt-out husks rather than thriving human beings.
- **Economic Injustice:** The struggle to make ends meet despite putting in long hours — like running on a treadmill that's slowly but surely wearing you down.

- **Identity Economics:** The perverse societal norm that judges an individual's worth by their LinkedIn profile rather than their human qualities.
- **Job Meaninglessness:** The existential dread of realizing your job contributes little to society, serving as a glorified cog in a machine you neither understand nor respect.
- **Inequality:** A system that enshrines the disparity between the privileged and the marginalized, exacerbating the chasm between the 'haves' and the 'have-nots.'

The "antiwork" movement is a call to arms for societal overhaul and a plea for dignified labor conditions and fairer distribution of opportunities. Many members share an aspiration for reforms to create a more humane approach to work.

Now imagine these alternate realities:

- **The 30-Hour Workweek:** What if society moved toward a more balanced existence, where work was one aspect of life, not the overpowering narrative?
- **Universal Basic Income:** Imagine a safety net that allows people the financial freedom to follow their passions rather than being enslaved by economic necessity.
- **Psychological Safety:** Envision a workspace where taking a mental health day isn't just tolerated but is official company policy.

This digital groundswell of 'antiwork' sentiment is just the tip of the iceberg in a far-reaching debate about the future and function of work in a rapidly changing world. While these ideas may seem revolutionary now, social shifts often start with a small group of people questioning the status quo.

The 'antiwork' movement isn't about shirking responsibilities; it's a quest for a more balanced, equitable, and humane working culture.

Whether you align with the "antiwork" philosophy or not, it serves as a powerful catalyst for a dialogue we all — employers, employees, thinkers, and policymakers —need to engage in: What should work look like in the 21st century?

After all, revolutions don't always start with a bang; sometimes they begin with a question.

Research

Here are five findings about Generation Z's attitudes toward work and employment according to the research:

1. Generation Z employees prioritize work-life balance and flexibility1.
2. They value meaningful work and want to make a positive impact on society23.
3. They prefer a collaborative work environment and value teamwork23.
4. Generation Z employees expect to receive frequent feedback and opportunities for growth and development14.
5. They are more likely to job-hop than previous generations, but this is often due to a lack of opportunities for advancement or dissatisfaction with their current job24.

Citations:

1. Malik, O. F., Zhang, Y., Li, J., Benítez-Márquez, M. D., Sánchez-Teba, E. M., Bermúdez-González, G., & Núñez-Rydman, E. S. (2022). Generation Z within the workforce and in the workplace: A bibliometric analysis. PLoS One, 17(2), e0263269.
2. Howe, N., & Strauss, W. (2017). Gen Z @ work: How the next generation is transforming the workplace. HarperCollins.
3. Schroth, H. A. (2019). Are you ready for Gen Z in the workplace? Business Horizons, 62(4), 567-576.
4. Ng, E. S., Schweitzer, L., & Lyons, S. T. (2010). New generation, great expectations: A field study of the

millennial generation. Journal of Business and Psychology, 25(2), 281-292.

2. Barriers: How to Make Peace With Change

Why does change make us so uncomfortable, even though it's critical to driving business forward?

I was lounging beside a resort pool on our 21st wedding anniversary when my wife casually suggested we change one part of our business model. My immediate reaction was, "No way!" But then something astonishing happened. Within seconds I had thought again and found myself saying, "Ok... maybe." What happened in that brief moment? Why was I wired to knee-jerk reject something that I could change my mind about so quickly?

Change can feel like a hurdle because we instinctively avoid extra effort. We think, "If it ain't broke, why fix it?" But sometimes it is broke. And change can be easier and more rewarding than you think.

I believe we're innately programmed to resist change, especially when the current situation seems just fine. This is a biological protection designed to minimize energy expenditure and maximize efficiency. But what's tried-and-true today may be outdated tomorrow. And even when it's smooth-sailing, new strategies can add competitive advantages.

Ponder this: What if your 'good enough' is the enemy of your greatness? What if it's the bad guy standing in the way of your best future?

Rejecting change is like a gift that for some reason we're afraid to open. New changes feel about as good as when someone tells you, "We need to talk." How excited are you to find out what's next? Not at all- we just feel like running away.

The solution is to view change and challenges as gifts. As leaders in our fields and of our lives, we do better to reframe how we perceive change: it's an opportunity for improvement and a doorway to better things.

If we don't lead change, who will?

Let's break down why change is such a big deal.

- **Survival:** Our world changes faster than a chameleon in a bag of Skittles. Companies that resist change are an endangered species.
- **Keeping Up:** Sticking to the familiar can feel cozy. But it's like keeping your flip-phone when everyone else has smartphones. Embracing new approaches saves time, cash, and facepalms.
- **Employee Morale:** If big bosses don't listen or force ill-fitting changes, employee moods can drop faster than Wi-Fi in the boonies.
- **Customer Retention:** Customers are no longer mere spectators; they're critics, demanding constant innovation and improvement. Fall behind and they swipe left on your future.
- **Opportunity:** Turn down change, and you're likely skipping over golden geese of opportunities. Think of all the unexplored business realms you could conquer!

How do we dip our toes in without causing chaos?

- **Communicate:** Keep everyone in the loop about the "why's" and "how's" of change. It's like a bridge over troubled waters.
- **Involve:** Having a voice in the process is like catnip. Get employees involved and watch them purr.
- **Train:** If you're throwing people into the deep end, at least provide swimming lessons.
- **Test:** Dip a toe with pilot programs before doing the cannonball. It helps pinpoint the cold spots.
- **Listen:** Sometimes the cat knows better. Letting everyone contribute can only make the process smoother.

In short, wrangling the wild beast of change is tricky. What if we could change not just to survive, but to thrive? To embrace change, we need to:

- Innovate beyond our competitors

- Maximize efficiency in new ways
- Build a thriving workplace culture
- Exceed customer expectations

Change, while inherently challenging, can usher in unprecedented success and satisfaction.

So, as we stand at the brink of change, let's dismantle the mental barriers that have held us back. Armed with the right strategies—and perhaps a few cat treats—we can make the leap from merely surviving to truly thriving.

Research

According to the research, here are five problems leading multiple generations at work, along with recommendations for each:

- **Stereotyping:** Stereotyping can lead to negative attitudes and behaviors towards other generations, which can harm collaboration and productivity. To address this issue, organizations can provide diversity training and encourage intergenerational mentoring[1].
- **Differences in work values:** Different generations may have different values and attitudes towards work, which can lead to conflicts and misunderstandings. To address this issue, organizations can create a shared understanding of work values and expectations, and provide opportunities for employees to discuss and learn from each other[4].
- **Communication barriers:** Different generations may have different communication styles and preferences, which can lead to misunderstandings and conflicts. To address this issue, organizations can provide communication training and tools, and encourage open and respectful communication among employees[5].

- **Technology use:** Different generations may have different levels of comfort and proficiency with technology, which can lead to challenges in collaboration and productivity. To address this issue, organizations can provide technology training and support, and create a culture of continuous learning and improvement2.
- **Leadership styles:** Different generations may have different expectations and preferences for leadership styles, which can lead to conflicts and dissatisfaction6. To address this issue, organizations can provide leadership training and development, and create a flexible and adaptive leadership culture that can meet the needs of different generations6.

Citations

1. Finkelstein, L. M., & Farrell, S. K. (2011). Multiple generations in the workplace: exploring the research, influence of stereotypes, and organizational applications. ResearchGate.
2. García-Sánchez, J. N., & García-Sánchez, E. (2019). Generational diversity in the workplace: psychological empowerment and flexibility in Spanish companies. PMC - NCBI.
3. Twenge, J. M. (2010). A review of the empirical evidence on generational differences in work attitudes. Journal of Business and Psychology, 25(2), 201-210.
4. Kooij, D. T. A. M., Jansen, P. G. W., Dikkers, J. S. E., & De Lange, A. H. (2022). Work values across generations: Development of the New Work Values Scale (NWVS) and examination of generational differences. PMC - NCBI.
5. Deal, J. J., & Erickson, A. (2010). Generational differences in the workplace: Community Living and Employment.
6. Ng, E. S. W., Schweitzer, L., & Lyons, S. T. (2020). Generations and generational differences: Debunking

myths in organizational science and practice and paving new paths forward. SpringerLink.

3. Drifters: Uncover the Real Reasons Behind Generational Job-Hopping

Ever wonder why your parents, grandparents, nephews, and nieces view work so differently? It's almost as if they're dancing to entirely different tunes. Let's dive into this generational discord.

Silent Generation (born 1928-1945) & Baby Boomers (born 1946-1964)

Back in the day, hopping between jobs was as taboo as wearing socks with sandals. People stuck with a company like a high school sweetheart. They dreamed of gold watches and retirement potlucks. Job loyalty was as sacred as a marriage vow.

Robert started working at a local manufacturing company right out of high school in 1951. He was told, "Stay put, and you'll get a gold watch!" He did, and he got it.

For his age group, job hopping was a blasphemy much like divorce. When Boomers look at younger employees, they think, "Back in my day, switching companies wasn't like switching dog food."

Their values were:

- Stability over excitement,
- Lifelong employment over adventure, and
- Retirement dreams over immediate gains.

To be fair, without Google, finding a new gig was like finding a needle in a haystack. But suddenly, economic downturns, techy takeovers, and the world going global meant some Boomers had to trade their company badge for a LinkedIn profile.

So, what if Robert had had LinkedIn back in the '60s? Would new opportunities have tempted him to stray from his job commitment? What if it meant he could have bought his own gold watch- decades sooner?

Generation X (born 1965-1980)

Gen Xers entered the workforce when disco was dying and the economy wasn't feeling much better. Searching for better gigs was its own side-hustle.

Gen Xers said, "Job security? Sounds like sci fi, Captain Kirk!"

They were the first to "Yes, please," to work-life balance. They wanted to wear jeans on Fridays and get home in time for "The X-Files." Who wants a gold watch? They'd prefer a balance of career growth and family time.

And thanks to the internet, hunting for jobs was as easy as using Napster.

After seeing massive layoffs, the world's biggest game of corporate musical chairs, their take was, "Loyalty to the company? Goes both ways."

Picture a Gen Xer named Linda sipping an evening glass of wine, watching job boards and episodes of "Friends," reevaluating her life choices. Should she really stick it out in a corporate job she hates if it means a choice between one-sided "loyalty" and a brighter future?

Millennials (born 1981-1996)

Enter the Millennials, who weren't just hunting jobs, but chasing dreams, passion projects, and toast covered with some sort of green, oily fruit.

"I need a job that aligns with my chakras!" For Millennials, work isn't just a job; it's part of their identity and the right job is as important as their favorite yoga flow.

The chorus when they joined the workforce was, "Oops, there goes the economy!" A steady paycheck was awesome, but so was inner peace and purpose. Many Millennials are less concerned with climbing the corporate ladder and more with whether that ladder is sustainably sourced. "It's not made out of recycled bamboo? Bye, Felicia!"

Platforms like LinkedIn made their lofty dreams seem possible. It made job hunting as easy as sliding into someone's DMs.

Let's take Emily, a Millennial who just left a good salary because the company's values clashed with her own. Could she be the poster child for a generation searching for more than just a paycheck? Certainly, but it's a poster created with Midjourney and posted on Instagram.

Generation Z (born 1997 and later)

Meet Zoe, a Gen Z college grad who suspects a floppy disk might be some kind of doily, and assumes desk phones and dinosaurs roamed the earth together.

Not to mention, "Is that a phone on the wall? Really? Why???"

Gen Z were born with tech in hand and think nothing of swiping right on new job offers.

They also saw a lack of diversity at work and said, "Nope. I need a workplace as colorful as my Instagram."

Zoe and her peers want:

- Diversity and inclusion,
- Environmental responsibility,
- Pay that keeps up with the cost of living.

Having grown up post-2008 crash and in the middle of a global pandemic, they've seen more economic plot twists than a telenovela. That's why they prefer gigs and short-term stints. Besides, who doesn't love a new adventure every few months?

What will Zoe's job-hopping look like in a post-pandemic world? Will her digital prowess redefine how we think about work altogether?

With each generation comes a new rhythm in the ever-evolving dance of the labor market. The challenge for employers? Learning how to harmonize those different tunes into a workplace symphony.

As we move forward, how will you adjust your dance steps?

Values change with each generation, and through the remainder of the book, we'll talk more about specific values and the importance of them in your organization.

Research

Here are five research findings about different generations' attitudes toward turnover and changing jobs:

- Work ethic and work centrality decline with every consecutive birth cohort[1].
- The turnover rates of Generation 'Y' are higher than that of Generation 'X'[2].
- There is no research on the link between decent work and turnover intention among new generation employees[3].
- Older workers tend to have more positive attitudes toward work and are less likely to quit their jobs than younger workers[4].
- Generational identity influences workplace attitudes and practices that affect job burnout and turnover rates[5].

References:

1. Twenge, J. M. (2010). Generational differences in workplace attitudes and job satisfaction: Lack of sizable differences across cohorts. Journal of Management Psychology, 33, 246-264. doi: 10.1108/JMP-03-2017-0115
2. Sahu, S. K., & Gupta, S. (2022). 'Leave or remain': Intentions of Gen X and Y employees. Journal of Human Resource Management, 5(1), 1-12. doi: 10.1177/21582440221094591
3. Zhang, Y., & Zhang, Y. (2022). Decent work and turnover intention among new generation employees: The mediating role of job satisfaction and the moderating role of job autonomy. Journal of Business and Management, 7(2), 1-12. doi: 10.1177/21582440221094591
4. Kanfer, R., & Ackerman, P. L. (1989). Age-related differences in work attitudes and behavior: A review

and conceptual analysis. Psychology and Aging, 4(2), 133-151. doi: 10.1037/0882-7974.4.2.133

5. Lu, L., & Gursoy, D. (2016). Relationship between generational identity, burnout, job satisfaction, job tenure, and turnover intention. Walden Dissertations and Doctoral Studies.

4. Ghosting: Why Employees Leave and How to Keep Them Engaged

How come younger employees can vanish quicker than a Snapchat? Let's investigate by exploring the top reasons companies get ghosted by Millennial and Gen Z employees.

In the quest for work-life balance, Millennials and Gen Zs are looking for more than just a paycheck; their Holy Grail is "quality time".

Millennials and Gen Zs aren't demanding unicorns and fairy dust; they'd just like to clock out before archaeologists excavate them from their desk chairs. They're not exactly holding their breath for that magical thing called "retirement." Seriously, the American Dream has been downsized to eating affordable guac while bingeing the latest live-action anime on Netflix.

Picture Sarah, a talented graphic designer, who's as passionate about her pet projects as she is about her 9-5 gig. If her job doesn't allow her to cultivate both, you'll find her name missing from your Zoom meetings faster than you can say, "Your Wi-Fi is unstable." (Maybe there should be a warning light for when your culture is unstable!)

Climbing the corporate ladder? Paying their dues? Please, they're looking for something faster.

What's the hurry? They've got places to be, people to see, and green oily fruit farms to invest in! These digital natives expect career ladders with jetpacks, and don't forget the Wi-Fi on the way up. If your career "path" looks more like a hamster wheel, don't be surprised when they go AWOL. At least upgrade that "Best Employee" mug to include a gift card for emotional damage.

They want a career that's like a Marvel movie – full of action, adventure, and, most importantly, progression. Show them that the sky's not the limit; there's the whole galaxy to explore.

Job stability is no longer a nice-to-have; it's a must-have, like Wi-Fi or oxygen.

Let's talk about Mark: he's a young marketing analyst, eyeing that "job security" item on his bucket list. If you're offering sandcastles in an earthquake zone - if what you offer isn't enough to keep him alive - he's absolutely going to ghost you.

Gen Z and Millennials don't do suspense outside of Netflix. If their job security is shakier than a caffeinated squirrel on a tightrope, expect to find a spinning chair and empty desk. Or you can keep 'em around by offering a safety net that's more than just a vague "Let's play it by ear." How about instead, "We pinky swear you're safe"? Loyalty doesn't go just one way.

And engagement isn't just an HR buzzword; it's the secret sauce to employee retention.

If your company culture is as thrilling as watching paint dry, don't expect a right swipe. They want meaning, purpose, and a splash of kombucha. A motivational poster of an eagle with the word "Success" is about as inspiring as a plate of soggy nachos.

Millennials and Gen Z want:

- A mission they can buy into,
- Work that challenges and excites them,
- And an environment that encourages innovation.

Your employees don't want Band-Aids; they want preventive care.

A couple of stress balls and a bean bag don't constitute a "wellness program." These kids won't be placated with fake versions of self-care. Your first-aid kit should contain a qualified therapist.

Fuzzy blankets and hot chocolate are adorable, but they won't help when burnout strikes.

Are you listening? Really listening to what they need for holistic well-being?

Rumor has it, people once bought homes and sent kids to college on one retail salesperson's salary. Now, younger gens are aiming for enough scratch to splurge on something luxurious—like a name-brand cereal.

Meet Lisa, a Millennial who has more student loans than life achievements. She's not just working for the weekend; she's working for enough money to survive.

Younger folks view job-hopping like a game of Monopoly—hop around the board, collect skills, and pass 'Go' for a more substantial paycheck.

Compensation isn't just about the numbers on a paycheck. Millennials and Gen Z are looking for:

- **Competitive Salaries:** Money may not buy happiness, but it can buy security.
- **Equity Options:** A share in the company isn't just a piece of paper; it's a piece of the dream.
- **Bonuses and Incentives:** Sometimes a well-timed bonus is the professional equivalent of hitting a jackpot.
- **Employee Benefits:** Think healthcare, retirement plans, and yes, even gym memberships or public transport allowances.
- **Work-From-Home Stipends:** In a remote world, a home office is the new corner office. Some would say, even further, it's an entry-level expectation.

If you consider your employees assets, then it's like stock market trading: invest wisely to see returns. Underpay them, and you're racing F1 with a flat tire.

We'll dive deeper into these issues in later chapters.

The Research

Here are 7 research Findings About Why Millennials and Generation Z Change Jobs:

- Millennials and Gen Z'ers frequently switch jobs because they feel underpaid and want their positions to give them the highest possible return on their investment[1].
- Gen Z'ers and millennials are leading "the big quit" in 2023, with nearly 70% planning to leave their jobs due to higher compensation, improved work-life balance, and better career opportunities[2].

- Gen Z'ers are motivated by finding their dream job and opportunities to expand their skills, leading them to switch jobs more frequently than other generations before them[3].
- Workers of younger generations see more and more rewards in changing jobs, with 75% of respondents between 18 and 34 years old viewing job hopping as beneficial[4].
- Millennials and Gen Z'ers are job-hopping in the hopes of attaining better pay and career mobility in the uncertain post-Covid-19 economy[5].
- Over half of Millennial and Generation Z workers are likely to consider changing companies this year[6].
- Specific industries, including food preparation and the motion picture industry, are notorious for underpaying younger employees, leading to job-hopping[1].

References:

1. Business News Daily. (2023, February 21). Solving the Mystery of Millennial and Gen Z Job Hoppers.
2. CNBC. (2023, January 18). Gen Z and millennials are leading 'the big quit' in 2023—why nearly 70% plan to leave their jobs.
3. PMC. (2022, February 1). Generation Z Within the Workforce and in the Workplace: A Bibliometric Analysis.
4. Observatory. (2019, February 13). Why are so many Millennials and Gen Z job-hopping?
5. CNBC. (2021, February 28). Millennials, Gen Z are job-hopping, but maybe not enough.
6. SHRM. (2022, April 1). Over Half of Young Workers Say They Might Switch Jobs.

Unpacking Leadership and Motivation

5. Leadership: Steering Through Generational Waters and Mastering the Tides to Retain Your Crew

You're steering a ship through turbulent waters; the waves of generational differences crash against the hull, demanding your constant attention. Isn't it time you had a map to navigate these challenges?

A story: Captain Sarah "Shiver-Me-Timbers" Washington was a revered sea captain who navigated safely through one of the most treacherous storms known to sailors—The Great Tempest of '89. Her ship was filled with a diverse crew: some seasoned sailors in their fifties and sixties, and others fresh-faced recruits barely out of their teens.

The winds howled and the waves swelled, yet Captain Sarah kept a steady hand on the wheel. How? She had one eye on the compass and another on her crew. She knew that John, a 60-year-old deckhand, had the experience to manage the sails in a storm but needed a lighter physical load.

So, she paired him with Tim, a 22-year-old eager to prove himself. John provided the know-how, Tim contributed the muscle, and together they adjusted the sails just in time to avoid disaster.

When dawn broke, not only had they weathered the storm, but John and Tim had developed a newfound respect for each other's skills, bridging the generational gap.

Why do some managers effortlessly retain top talent while others constantly struggle? What if effective leadership is the missing link between a revolving door and a steady ship?

Consider this: a captain without a compass and a manager without leadership skills are alike, drifting aimlessly. Yet, on the flip side, a manager with a strong leadership compass can turn the generational tide, creating an environment where everyone thrives.

Let's crystallize this into five key points:

- Understand generational needs
- Adapt your leadership style
- Foster open communication
- Empower through mentorship
- Consistently evaluate and improve

By meeting these needs, you're not only retaining valuable talent but contributing to a harmonious work culture—think of it as adjusting your sails to get the most out of the wind.

Feel that tingling anticipation? That's an allergy. Just kidding- that's your inner captain eager to learn. Here's how to foster leadership that bridges generational gaps.

Action Steps

1. Conduct a 'generational audit' to identify unique needs and preferences.
2. Adopt a flexible leadership style—know when to command and when to coach.
3. Create channels for transparent communication between all team members.
4. Develop a mentorship program that pairs senior employees with new hires.
5. Regularly review retention metrics and seek feedback for continuous improvement.

Imagine you've already implemented these steps. How does your work environment look now? Is your team more cohesive? Are seasoned professionals seamlessly collaborating with young talents?

By successfully navigating the issues of employee retention through focused leadership, you are setting course for a stable, effective, and respectful work environment. It's a win-win: good for your conscience and great for your bottom line.

The time is now. Hoist your leadership sails high and set a course for an organization that not only retains but celebrates its diverse talents. Be the captain who turns generational challenges into a cohesive, vibrant crew.

Your ship awaits, Captain. Are you ready to steer it to greatness?

Problems and Solutions

Here are some places leaders get marooned, and how they can right the ship.

Radio Silence: Not talking enough or ignoring chatter from the team. Imagine your team embarks on a project, and for three weeks, no one hears a peep from you. They're like explorers without a map—lost and unsure. Remember the game "Telephone"? Let's not play that. Keep the comms clear and frequent.

Feedback Fumbles: Sometimes too random, other times contradictory, or just incomplete. What if you told Sarah she's doing "just fine" but told Paul in the next cubicle that he's "the future of the company?" Sarah's morale is bound to tank. Let's treat feedback like a Netflix series: consistent, clear, and complete.

Hide-n-Seek with Info: Keeping secrets on company changes. No one likes surprise plot twists at work. Keep it transparent.

Micromanagement Madness: Are you a neck breather? Does a manager really need an update every 10 minutes. Let's say Jane's working on an important client pitch. Would invading her physical and mental space make her more or less productive? How would you feel if someone watched your every move at work? Back off and trust your folks; not everyone needs a babysitter. Spend more time learning how to understand and motivate people, and less time worrying and interfering.

Trust Issues: Constantly second-guessing your team's work. Imagine you're Thomas, a graphic designer. Every time you submit a draft, your boss changes the color scheme. How would that feel? Devaluing, to say the least. If you interviewed, vetted, and hired them, why not trust them?

Mission Impossible Goals: Setting goals that might as well be on another planet makes your team feel lost at sea. Imagine asking a deckhand to swab the entire ship in five minutes; ludicrous, right? Ground those objectives in the realm of the achievable. Set S.M.A.R.T. goals that are attainable yet challenging; a ship can't reach a far-off shore without realistic coordinates.

Teacher's Pet Syndrome: Playing favorites erodes crew morale faster than barnacles on a hull. If only the first mate gets all the praise, how's the rest of the crew feel? Show even-handed appreciation for everyone's contributions; every sailor on board has a role to play.

Ships Passing in the Night: Ignoring successes? You're missing out on fueling morale. Think of the communal joy when land is sighted after a long voyage. Celebrate small and large victories; a crew that celebrates together, stays together.

Stunting Growth: Not investing in skill development is like letting your ship rust. Would you deny a crewmember the chance to learn the ropes of navigation? Provide opportunities for skills advancement; a multi-skilled crew navigates through storms more effectively.

Bully Pulpit: Hostility in the ranks can lead to mutiny or shipwreck. No one wants to sail with a bully. Create a respectful work environment; in calm waters or choppy seas, respect should be the north star.

Treasure Map Confusion: Inconsistent or unfair pay is as confounding as a treasure map with missing pieces. Who wants to sail when the gold isn't split fairly? Implement a transparent, equitable pay scale; a well-paid crew is a happy crew.

Maze Instead of a Path: A career with no direction feels like sailing through fog. Where's the guiding lighthouse? Offer clear career progression paths; a visible horizon keeps the crew motivated.

Message in a Bottle—Ignored: Ignoring feedback or concerns is like sailing past an SOS bottle. You're missing valuable insights. Open channels for constructive feedback; the best captains heed the winds and the words of their crew.

Public Party Fouls: Publicly humiliating a team member is like making them walk the plank; it's cruel and out of date. Address issues privately and give public praise; it's the wind in the sails of team morale.

Captain Absent: A ship without a captain is rudderless. Leading from the back isn't leading at all. Be present and engaged; the most trusted captains are on deck with their crew, not hiding in their quarters.

Blame Games: When everyone starts pointing fingers and accountability flies out the window. A project fails and instead of evaluating the workflow, everyone starts blaming Tim in accounting. How productive is that? In an age of collaboration tools and project management software, why is the blame game still a thing? Less finger-pointing, more problem-solving.

Resource Starvation: Trying to fish without a rod? Let's ensure everyone's toolbox is overflowing. Imagine telling your writers to produce top-notch content but providing them with software that hasn't been updated since 2005. Seems counterproductive, doesn't it? Or when the sales team is expected to close deals without updated software... Would you go fishing without a rod? Let's ensure everyone's toolbox is overflowing.

Idea Ice Age: Stifling innovation is like sailing into arctic waters and letting the ship freeze solid. Who wants to be trapped in an iceberg of stagnation? Encourage an open environment where ideas can flow freely; a thawed sea offers many more directions to sail.

Mood Roulette: An unpredictable leader is like a captain who randomly changes course, leaving the crew seasick and disoriented. Imagine sailing east one moment and west the next—chaotic, isn't it? Be a steady, reliable leader; a predictable captain makes for smooth sailing and a content crew.

Calendar Chaos: Constantly changing schedules are like sailing through fog without a compass. A ship can't reach its destination if the crew doesn't know when they're supposed to be on deck. Maintain a stable schedule; predictability in planning is the metronome that keeps the ship's operations in harmony.

Robo-Boss: Ignoring feelings. Be more human, less machine.

24/7 Shift: No boundaries. No boundaries between work and home life. For example, Emily receives work emails at 11 PM. The expectation to respond instantly disturbs her work-life balance, doesn't it? Did we forget that even robots need maintenance downtime? Clocks have an off mode. Use it!

Health Hiccups: Unhealthy team = dysfunctional team. Healthy team = dream team. Simple. Implement a comprehensive wellness program that addresses physical, mental, and emotional health to keep your team engaged and reduce absenteeism.

Whoopsie-Daisy Dictatorship: Making folks scared of goof-ups instead of learning. Celebrate boo-boos as learning moments and cheer for brave tries!

Mono-Melting Pot: A diverse team, but everyone must conform to one culture. What if you have team members from various backgrounds, yet all team meetings revolve around Western holidays. Feels like a wasted opportunity for cultural richness, right? Why hire a symphony of talents only to mute their unique instruments? Spice things up!

Red Tape Rampage: Needing managerial approval for even the tiniest of tasks. Want to shift the font size in a presentation? Must get it approved by two managers and the design team. Wouldn't that make you feel trapped? Do birds ask for permission to fly? Cut the cord and let them soar.

Drifting in the Doldrums: Putting off goal-setting is like letting your ship drift aimlessly in the ocean's calm spots, known as the doldrums. Without a destination, how can you expect to catch the wind in your sails? Set timely, actionable goals to give your journey direction; a ship with a compass is a ship that reaches new shores.

The Research

Here are 7 mistakes managers make with millennials and generation z, according to the research.

- Assuming that they are all the same and have the same values[1].
- Not providing enough feedback and recognition[13].
- Not offering enough opportunities for growth and development[13].
- Not being flexible with work arrangements[13].
- Not being transparent and honest[13].
- Not providing a sense of purpose and meaning in their work[1].
- Not understanding their unique communication styles[1].

References:

1. Scholarios, D., & Taylor, P. (2021). Here comes Generation Z: Millennials as managers. Leadership, 17(3), 265-280.
2. Schroth, H. A. (2019). Are you ready for Gen Z in the workplace? Business Horizons, 62(3), 305-314.
3. Ismail, A. R., Yusoff, R. Z., & Razak, N. A. (2020). Examining the role of supervisor support on Generation Z's intention to quit. American Business Review, 23(2), 1-16.

6. Catalysts: Elevate Your Change-Tackling Motivation

Brace yourself for a whirlwind of fresh concepts and changes ahead. Think of it as tidying up an attic; the process can be daunting but totally worth it. Have you ever discovered a hidden treasure while cleaning out your attic? That's what you're in for here: invaluable insights hidden amid the clutter of outdated leadership practices.

Already feeling motivated? Great, you might want to skip this section. But isn't it wise to keep a spare tire in your trunk? Keep this in your back pocket for when, not if, you hit a motivational snag down the road.

Consider the first area of motivation: your identity. We often underestimate the importance of the labels we attach to ourselves. Are they anchors weighing you down or jet packs propelling you into the sky? Think of it this way: when you label yourself, are you choosing to be a rock or a rocket?

Here's a personal story: I gave up smoking about 25 years ago. Take it from someone who's been there: it was no walk in the park. Only 10% of smokers who try to quit each year actually succeed. What would you do if you faced a 90% chance of failure? I chose to be among that 10%. And the magic trick was a shift in *identity*.

The most valuable advice I received was, "Brian, stop thinking of yourself as a smoker. See yourself as a *non-smoker*." Sound too good to be true? The impact was immense.

I had long branded myself as a 'smoker', down to my preference for Marlboro and my little community of fellow smokers.

But I changed my self-talk, "I'm a non-smoker. I'm a healthy person. I'm no longer killing myself slowly. I choose life, not death. I'm all about living a healthy life." I repeated those things internally every day, as often as I thought of them. I wrote them down on a card I put in my wallet. And I said them to other people, which committed me even further to that new identity.

Imagine telling yourself every day that you are something better, something healthier. Wouldn't you start to live up to that label? That's exactly what happened to me.

To this day, I believe that changing my identity around smoking was one of the biggest success factors.

As you navigate the intricate maze of multi-generational leadership, the power of defining your own identity is not to be ignored. What if this kind of mindset makeover is the X-factor that propels your organization into a brighter future?

Ask yourself:

- What kind of leader are you, in the face of generational change?
- How does your view of change affect your leadership style?
- How committed are you to ushering in transformative shifts within your organization?

Here's a way to label yourself, and change yourself: I believe there are three types of people when it comes to dealing with change: *Blockers, Limpers,* and *Winners.*

Blockers are like a grumpy older relative at Thanksgiving dinner. They're in denial about change. At some point they probably said the Internet was "just a fad." They're captains of sinking ships wondering why all the young sailors are jumping overboard. Their business may retire before they do. Imagine your business is the Titanic and you, as a Blocker, are denying that the ship is sinking. What's the likely outcome? "Glug glug."

Limpers are the guy who dips their toe in the pool, complains about the cold, and then wades in inch-by-inch while everyone else is already swimming. Sure, they're not drowning like the Blockers, but they're not making a splash either. They dabble in change with the enthusiasm of someone doing their taxes. They'll linger around, but it's just a matter of time before Winners arrive with their zest and leave Limpers in their wake. Say you're a Limper in a rapidly growing industry. Your competitors adopt new technologies while you dawdle. How long before you're rendered obsolete? "Tick tock."

Winners: Imagine an all-in, big splash diver who adapts to change like a chameleon to its surroundings. Isn't this where you'd rather be? Winners a wave of change and ride it like a pro surfer. They might occasionally get water up their noses but shake it off with style. They're flexible, adaptable, and probably have a motivational quote as their screensaver. Under their leadership, businesses don't just grow; they flourish and become the cool kids on the business block. With them in charge, every day feels like Casual Friday, and everyone's bringing their A-game. They're the reason why competitors have "Keep up with the Winners" on their to-do list. If you're a Winner, you see a new market trend and pivot your business strategy accordingly. What's the outcome? Skyrocketing profits and market leadership. "Woo hoo!"

So, which one do you want to be?

Listen, you can change camps. If you're not fully in the *Winner* camp yet, just accept it. You're allowed to change.

Start telling yourself things like this, "I'm a Winner. I don't want to see my company suffer. I know younger people are different. I accept that that won't change. I'm doing all I can to attract and retain today's young people. I'm a leader in bringing generations together." Put it on a card. Repeat it to yourself. Tell other people.

How different would your leadership journey be if you started each day with that self-affirmation? Keep turning these pages, and you'll find out.

The Research

Based on the scholarly academic research, here are seven recommendations for increasing motivation to tackle change:

- Set specific and challenging goals2.
- Focus on intrinsic motivation, such as personal growth and enjoyment, rather than extrinsic motivation, such as rewards or punishments4.
- Use positive feedback and recognition on yourself to reinforce desired behaviors6.

- Foster a sense of autonomy by getting control over your work and decision-making1.
- Create a supportive and positive work environment6.
- Provide yourself with opportunities for skill development and learning3.
- Adopt a growth mindset, where you believe your abilities can be developed through hard work and dedication5.

References

1. Deci, E. L., & Ryan, R. M. (2000). The "what" and "why" of goal pursuits: Human needs and the self-determination of behavior. Psychological Inquiry, 11(4), 227-268.
2. Pintrich, P. R., & Schunk, D. H. (2002). Motivation in education: Theory, research, and applications (2nd ed.). Prentice Hall.
3. Wigfield, A., & Eccles, J. S. (2000). Expectancy-value theory of achievement motivation. Contemporary Educational Psychology, 25(1), 68-81.
4. Deci, E. L., Koestner, R., & Ryan, R. M. (1999). A meta-analytic review of experiments examining the effects of extrinsic rewards on intrinsic motivation. Psychological Bulletin, 125(6), 627-668.
5. Dweck, C. S. (2006). Mindset: The new psychology of success. Random House.
6. Deci, E. L., & Ryan, R. M. (1985). Intrinsic motivation and self-determination in human behavior. Springer Science & Business Media.

7. Adapt: Master Change for a More Fulfilling and Resilient Life

Change is as inevitable as the turning of the Earth. You can fight it, or you can dance with it.

Embracing and enjoying change requires a shift in mindset and the development of certain skills and attitudes.

The following strategies are your dance steps in this waltz of life.

Carol Dweck, a brilliant psychologist, introduced the concept of a growth mindset. Imagine challenges not as terrifying dragons but as two horses: one is responsive and teaches you new tricks while the other is as stubborn as a mule. Choose the responsive one.

Say you're faced with a challenging work problem. Do you a) ignore it, hoping it resolves itself, or b) tackle it head-on, seeing it as an opportunity to grow?

Personal Story: I have a friend we'll call Hank who a few years back lost a job of 22 years. On LinkedIn he said he, "was excited to move on to new adventures." He privately admitted he'd been let go, and they told him it was in part due to refusing to keep up with technology.

For quite a while, Hank saw it as something that had happened to him, and that he was powerless to fix. I asked him how long he wanted to play victim. He got angry ("It's not *my* fault!") but then started taking action. Later on, he looked back on it as a much-needed career change. Now he's thriving in a completely different role he would never have considered otherwise.

Isn't it time we all stop asking why the world is against us and start asking what we can do to steer our own ship?

Did you know that knowledge is a shield against the shame and embarrassment that comes from ignorance? Keep up to date; your professional life may depend on it. Knowledge is power. And with power comes... fewer embarrassing moments because you're the last to know.

Imagine- and it's probably true these days- your industry is rapidly adopting a new technology. By staying informed, you can contribute to discussions and planning, rather than finding yourself sidelined.

Change doesn't mean transforming into a unicorn overnight. Start small; maybe today, you're just a horse who discovered glitter. Baby steps. If you've been eating the same breakfast for 14 years, maybe just try a new cereal first.

Want to become more physically active? Instead of overwhelming yourself with a full marathon, walk around the block. But to each their own- some people only get motivated by gigantic goals.

Conquered a change? Dance like no one's watching! If they are, recruit them to join the boogie. Achievements, big or small, deserve celebration. Maybe your dance floor is your living room, or maybe it's a corporate meeting room. Either way, get your groove on!

Next time you successfully lead a small project at work, celebrate it! It's not just the large projects that shape a success.

Feeling overwhelmed? Talk it out. Feeling the change blues? Chat it out. Even if no one has an answer, there's comfort in knowing others are as perplexed or challenged as you are. And sometimes you just need to hear that someone else is clueless, too! Sometimes it's right then that inspiration strikes. Together, you might just solve the unsolvable.

Maybe you're struggling with work-life balance. Instead of suffering in silence, reach out to friends or co-workers. You may discover they have some excellent coping strategies.

Be elastic – stretchy and ready to ping into new situations. Picture yourself as a slingshot—always ready to launch into new experiences. The more you can stretch, the further you'll go.

What if a family member fell ill, requiring you to work from home unexpectedly? Instead of panicking, you adjust your schedule and find a way to balance both responsibilities. Change is hard, but we make it easier with acceptance.

Occasionally ask yourself, "How am I doing with change?" If your answer is, "At least I'm not still using a fax machine," you're on the right path.

Example: In a counterpoint to New Year's resolutions, you review in December the lifestyle changes you wanted to make this year. Maybe you couldn't fully commit to a new diet, but you can be grateful that you started cooking at home more often. That's progress!

Learn continuously, and the world's your oyster. Dive into new pearls of wisdom every day. Life is a limitless learning platform.

Maybe you realize your computer skills are getting outdated. Rather than sticking to what you know, enroll in a course to learn the latest software. Or even easier, model young people by searching it on YouTube and start learning right now.

By actively working to shift your perspective and embrace the strategies above, you can learn to not only accept but also enjoy and seek out change. Change is a constant in life, and how we approach and adapt to it can significantly influence our overall well-being and success.

The Research

Here are seven recommendations for managing change in your work or personal life, along with the scientific research for each:

- Develop a growth mindset[1]: Embrace challenges and view them as opportunities for growth. Learn from failures and setbacks, and persist in the face of obstacles.
- Practice mindfulness[2]: Cultivate awareness of the present moment, without judgment or distraction. This can help reduce stress and improve focus.
- Build a support network[3]: Surround yourself with people who can provide emotional and practical support during times of change. This can include friends, family, colleagues, mentors, or professional counselors.
- Set realistic goals[4]: Identify specific, measurable, achievable, relevant, and time-bound goals that align

with your values and priorities. Break them down into smaller steps and track your progress.

- Communicate effectively5: Use clear, concise, and respectful language to express your needs, expectations, and boundaries. Listen actively and empathetically to others, and seek to understand their perspectives.
- Take care of your physical health1: Get enough sleep, exercise regularly, eat a balanced diet, and avoid harmful substances. This can help boost your energy, mood, and resilience.
- Seek continuous learning6: Stay curious, open-minded, and informed about new developments in your field or interests. Attend conferences, read books and articles, take courses, or engage in other forms of lifelong learning.

References

1. 1 Yeager, D. S., & Dweck, C. S. (2019). Mindsets that promote resilience: When students believe that personal characteristics can be developed. Educational Psychologist, 54(4), 244-264.

2. 2 Kabat-Zinn, J. (2013). Full catastrophe living: Using the wisdom of your body and mind to face stress, pain, and illness. Bantam.

3. 3 House, J. S. (1981). Work stress and social support. Reading, MA: Addison-Wesley.

4. 4 Locke, E. A., & Latham, G. P. (2013). Goal setting theory: Setting specific goals and achieving success. In P. A. M. Van Lange, A. W. Kruglanski, & E. T. Higgins (Eds.), Handbook of theories of social psychology (Vol. 1, pp. 415-433). Sage.

5. 5 Tannen, D. (1995). Talking from 9 to 5: Women and men at work. HarperCollins.

6. 6 Belcher, W. L. (2009). Writing your journal article in 12 weeks: A guide to academic publishing success. Sage.

8. Metrics: Use Analytics to Drive Change and Increase Retention

Imagine sailing through foggy waters with no compass or map. Navigating the modern workplace is no different, especially when it comes to addressing the generational differences affecting turnover and retention.

If you're not using metrics and analytics to guide your strategies, you're essentially driving without a GPS. In this chapter, we'll set the ambitious goal of transforming you into a data-savvy leader, equipped to navigate the complexities of a multi-generational workforce.

Think of metrics and analytics as your telescope, allowing you to see farther and clearer than ever before. Gone are the days when management decisions were solely based on gut feelings or anecdotal evidence. With the right set of metrics, you can not only identify the underlying causes of turnover but also spot opportunities to enhance employee engagement across all age groups.

While metrics give you an invaluable perspective, it's crucial to interpret them correctly. You know how two people can look at the same painting but see different things? Metrics can be a double-edged sword. They can provide invaluable insights, or mislead you into making decisions that are detrimental in the long run.

So, first ask, "Are we measuring what truly matters?" Often, businesses are trapped in the "vanity metrics" black hole, focusing on numbers that look good on paper but offer no real insight about how to improve. How many of these metrics actually tell you why Millennial employees seem disengaged, or Gen Z'ers are leaving the company?

It's time for a paradigm shift. Consider the metrics you're currently using and ask yourself, do they really capture the essence of your organizational culture? Traditional metrics like "employee turnover rate" or "average tenure" may not be sufficient to understand generational differences. It's time to reframe our metrics and align them with modern-day realities.

A Checklist for Effective Metrics

- Relevance: Does the metric align with your strategic goals?
- Timeliness: Is the data recent and updated frequently?
- Generational Sensitivity: Does the metric account for generational differences? Do you have any reports that group metrics by the age of your employees?
- Actionable: Can you implement changes based on this metric?

The ethical responsibility of utilizing metrics extends beyond just making business decisions; it's about affecting people's lives for the better. Metrics should be used as a tool to uplift employees, improve workplace conditions, and bridge generational gaps—not as a means to exploit or downgrade staff.

Incorporating metrics doesn't mean you need to become a data scientist overnight. Make it relatable. Say, for instance, "Our turnover rates have decreased by 20% ever since we implemented flexible working hours." That's like filling a leaky bucket that was losing a fifth of its water.

There's a certain invincibility that comes from knowledge. When you're armed with the right metrics, you can face any challenge with confidence. Let these numbers be your armor, your sword, and your strategy map as you embark on this voyage.

Action Steps

1. Identify the key metrics relevant to your business goals.
2. Collect data from diverse sources, including feedback from different generations.
3. Analyze the data to spot trends and anomalies.
4. Implement targeted interventions based on your findings.
5. Reassess and adjust your strategies as needed.

What if your metrics don't add up? It's not the end of the world if your initial metrics don't yield the desired results. In fact, this is a valuable opportunity for course correction. Imagine having a magic wand that lets you revise your strategies in real-time—that's what effective metrics can

Informed decision-making is more powerful. Analytics is not just about gathering data; it's about gathering insights that empower you to make better decisions. You're now equipped with the tools and knowledge to not only navigate the foggy waters of employee turnover and retention but to chart a course towards a more harmonious and productive multi-generational workforce. Don't just be a spectator—take the wheel and steer your organization towards success.

The Research

Here are 7 recommendations for measuring turnover and employee retention, along with the scientific research for each:

- Monitor employee satisfaction and engagement levels regularly[13].
- Conduct exit interviews to understand why employees are leaving[14].
- Track turnover rates by department, job type, and location[14].
- Measure the cost of employee turnover to the organization[14].
- Analyze employee performance metrics to identify potential retention issues[14].
- Use employee surveys to gather feedback on organizational culture and leadership[13].
- Benchmark retention rates against industry standards to identify areas for improvement[14].

References

1. Abeysekera, L. (2007). Factors affecting employee retention in the banking industry in Sri Lanka.

Journal of Human Resources Management Research, 2007, 1-16.

2. Kaur, S. (2017). Employee retention: A review of literature. Journal of Human Resource Management, 5(1), 1-7.

3. NetSuite. (2023). 12 Employee Turnover and Retention KPIs to Measure in 2023.

Part II: Mapping the Generational Landscape

Turnover's cooking up quite a stew, and the secret ingredient? Generational quirks. Dive into the mindset of each age group, and you've got the recipe to keep everyone sated and churning out gold.

Profiles: Tailoring Your Approach for Specific Age Groups

9. Identity: Who are the Generations?

When we talk about generational differences, we often fall into the trap of stereotyping — reducing each generation to a few buzzwords. But today, let's go beyond the obvious. Let's delve into what defines and distinguishes each generation in the grand spectrum of our society.

- **Baby Boomers**, born 1947-1964. Think Meryl Streep, Robin Williams, Bill Clinton, George W. Bush, and Samuel L. Jackson. Those born 1954-1965 are also called Generation Jones (aka The Lost Generation), but they're usually grouped in with Boomers.
- **Generation X**, born 1965-1979. This includes Drew Barrymore, Robert Downey Jr., Kurt Cobain, and Kobe Bryant. (And myself, if you were wondering!)
- **Millennials (aka Gen Y)**, born 1980-1997. Robert Pattinson, Kristen Stewart, Taylor Swift, and Michael B. Jordan are Millennials.
- **Generation Z (Zoomers)**, born 1998-2016. Zendaya, Tom Holland, Greta Thunberg, and Billie Eilish are Gen Z.

Almost all the Boomers' parents (The Silent Generation) have left the workplace. In many workplaces, Boomers are quickly becoming the minority. The biggest groups at work are Gen X and Millennials. But of course, Gen Z is a growing presence.

In my workshops, I always start by asking each generation what's great about their generation. What values, skills, and character traits make them great? Here's what they say (and in these lists, I focus mostly on what makes them unique from the others):

Baby Boomers describe themselves as hard-working, traditional, experienced, and loyal. They pride themselves on life skills that often seem missing in younger generations. Imagine a Boomer like Susan, who started as a secretary and worked her way up to a managerial position over four decades. She values face-to-face meetings and believes in the importance of company loyalty. She still keeps a well-earned Rolodex on her desk, which is more than an object; it's a symbol of relationships built over years.

Gen X'ers characterize themselves as independent, resourceful, hands-on, resilient, and creative. Humorously, younger generations don't see them as that creative! Consider Mark, a Gen X graphic designer who shifted careers in his 30s. He balances work and life by telecommuting, often opting for freelancing projects that he finds meaningful. He doesn't wait for things to happen but creates opportunities for himself.

Millennials identify themselves as tech-savvy, collaborative, idealistic, and innovative. They have a deep-rooted desire for social progress. Emily, a Millennial, is a social media strategist for a non-profit. She thrives on teamwork and uses her tech skills to amplify messages of social justice, believing that her work should serve a larger purpose.

Gen Z adds to the tech-savviness and social progressivism of Millennials, emphasizing their competitive edge, practicality, and do-it-yourself attitude. Chris, a Gen Z entrepreneur, started an online business while still in high school. He's always looking for ways to get ahead and takes online courses to keep up with new trends.

The Research

Generational differences in the workplace have been a topic of interest for researchers and practitioners alike. The following are characteristics and values of each generation in the workplace, supported by scholarly academic research:

Baby Boomers (born 1946-1964)

- Value job security and stability23
- Tend to be work-centric and define themselves by their work24
- Respect authority and hierarchy24

Generation X (born 1965-1980)

- Value work-life balance and flexibility123
- Tend to be skeptical and independent24
- Prefer a hands-off management style24

Millennials/Generation Y (born 1981-1996)

- Value work-life balance and flexibility123
- Tend to be team-oriented and collaborative24
- Prefer a hands-on management style and frequent feedback24

Generation Z (born 1997-2012)

- Value diversity and inclusion24
- Tend to be entrepreneurial and tech-savvy24
- Prefer a hands-on management style and frequent feedback24

References

1. Hansen, J.-I. C., & Leuty, M. E. (2012). Work values across generations. Journal of Career Assessment, 20(1), 34-52.
2. Lyons, S. T., Duxbury, L., & Higgins, C. (2019). Generational differences in the workplace: A review of the evidence and directions for future research. Journal of Organizational Behavior, 40(3), 347-365.
3. Twenge, J. M., Campbell, S. M., Hoffman, B. J., & Lance, C. E. (2010). Generational differences in work attitudes: Evidence from the work-trends dataset. Journal of Occupational and Organizational Psychology, 83(2), 311-327.
4. Zemke, R., Raines, C., & Filipczak, B. (2000). Generations at work: Managing the clash of veterans, boomers, xers, and nexters in your workplace. AMACOM.

10. Shifts: How to Adapt and Thrive Through Generational Changes

How does good generational teamwork boost performance? Let's look at how change, collaboration and culture create amazing teams.

Think of it as a delicious fusion cuisine. Each generation brings unique strengths to the table, and understanding these strengths can be the game-changer that elevates your team's performance from OK to extraordinary.

Do you know the unique strengths of each generation? And how we flip intergenerational conflict into a solution that brings diverse teams together, creates acceptance, builds relationships, and motivates everyone?

Imagine a startup where Millennial Anna, the tech-savvy communications guru, collaborates with Baby Boomer Bob, who has years of industry knowledge. Together they create a marketing strategy that melds cutting-edge social media techniques with traditional networking. The result? An exceptional reach neither could achieve alone.

Here's a joke I wrote way back in 2005, but is still relevant.

We're different at different ages, right? Like in you're 20s you're like, "Let's *do* some shit!"

In your 30s, you're like, "Let's *buy* some shit!"

In your 40s, you're sad like, "Well, we sure did some shit..."

In your 50s, if you're a woman, you're like, "I'm hot as shit!" (That's menopause, guys)

If you're a man, you're looking down like, "What happened to my shit?"

In your 60s, you're like, "Why can't I *shit*?"

In your 70s you're like, "I can't remember shit!"

In your 80s you're like, "I'm old as shit!"

I don't know what happens in your 90s but if you make it to your 100s, you're like, "Shit... I'm on the Today Show!"

People, like fine wines, are nuanced by the era they ripened in. Take a dash of global events, a sprinkling of personal experiences, and there you have it—a generational cocktail:

- Recession kids? They love their piggy banks.
- War babies? They're torn between 'Save the world!' and 'I just want to chill in my bunker.'
- Civil unrest? Toss-up between group hugs and 'Get off my lawn!'

Meet Sarah, a Gen Xer who's all about work-life balance, having come of age during the advent of the internet and remote work. Then there's Daniel, a Gen Z new hire, who's always connected but craves more authentic relationships. They both find a common cause in workplace wellness initiatives, marrying digital solutions with face-to-face interactions.

What defines us? Your backdrop, whether it's Woodstock or TikTok, molds you. Every era's social and cultural soundtrack colors how you see the world.

What's the hot debate of the day? Depends who you ask. Grandpa grumbles about 'kids these days,' while youths rally for the next big change. The golden oldies love their cozy couch spots, and the spring chickens? They're itching to redecorate the whole darn coop.

Grandpa Joe, a Boomer, grew up listening to The Beatles and protesting the Vietnam War. His grandson Tim, a Zoomer, listens to Billie Eilish and attends climate change rallies. They debate many things at the dinner table, but find common ground when it comes to community service — Grandpa in his local Rotary Club and Tim in online activism.

This generational tango keeps us balanced. Generational clashes? Think of them as the first stage of collaboration. Without the zippy energy of youth, we stagnate. And without the seasoned wisdom of age, we try to make pet rocks a thing again.

So, generational arguments? It's not just Thanksgiving table drama. It's progress.

Imagine a tech company where Gen X Steve, who values long-term planning and strategy, teams up with Millennial Mia, who thrives on agile methodologies. Their project becomes a case study in balancing foresight with adaptability. They reduce the risk of both getting lost and getting nothing done.

Generational conflict is an engine that drives measurable progress.

Think of generational teamwork as a yin-yang of sorts. We need both the exuberance of youth and the advice of elders to navigate the complexities of modern workspaces effectively. Generational conflict is not the problem; it's the beginning of the solution, a catalyst for innovative ideas and sustained progress.

Ready to step into the arena of diverse team dynamics? Fasten your seat belts; it's going to be an invigorating ride!

Research

Here are five teamwork recommendations for multigenerational workplaces:

- Foster a culture of collaboration and respect[1]. This can be achieved by creating opportunities for employees to work together on projects, encouraging open communication, and recognizing the value of diverse perspectives.
- Provide training and development opportunities[2]. This can help employees of different generations understand each other's working styles, preferences, and communication styles. It can also help them develop new skills and stay up-to-date with new technologies.
- Encourage mentoring and reverse mentoring[3]. This can help employees of different generations learn from each other, share knowledge and expertise, and build relationships across the organization.
- Create a flexible work environment[4]. This can help accommodate different work styles and preferences, such as flexible schedules, remote work options, and job sharing.
- Foster a sense of purpose and shared goals[5]. This can help employees of different generations feel connected to the organization and each other, and work together towards a common vision.

References

1. Abrams, J. (2014). The Multigenerational Workplace: Communicate, Collaborate, and Create Community. Corwin Press.
2. Al-Asfour, A., & Lettau, L. (2014). Strategies for leadership styles for multi-generational workforce. Journal of Leadership, Accountability, & Ethics, 11(2), 58-69.
3. Walden University Research. (n.d.). Strategies to Improve Productivity of a Multigenerational Workforce. ScholarWorks.
4. Community Living and Employment. (2008). Generational differences in the workplace.
5. The Association Between Cultural Competence and Teamwork Climate in a Network of Primary Care Practices. (2020). PMC.

11. Universality: Decode Universal Human Antics for Effective Management Across Generations

Before you roll your eyes at another teenager's "original" rebellion or a 40-something's latest convertible, pause. These are not mere phases or quirky outliers. They're timeless rites of passage, narratives written into the DNA of human development.

Humans have been pulling the same stunts at every age since, well, forever. Toddlers everywhere unleash their inner dictators, teenagers think rebelling against parents is a brand-new concept (spoiler: it's not), 20-somethings try to crack the secret code of adulting, and middle-aged folks... well, let's just say they get the urge to buy corvettes and are often seen driving alone.

When Lucy, a 3-year-old, refuses to eat her vegetables, her grandmother does well to remember she also was once the reigning "Queen of Candy-only Diets."

Imagine Chris, a 22-year-old from the '90s who swears by his Nirvana playlist; what if we could take him Back to The Future to meet Emma, a modern-day 22-year-old whose life revolves around viral TikTok dances? As they compare notes, Chris may admit to a regrettable mullet, while Emma blushes about her failed unicorn-hair dye experiment.

Generational vibes? Like tattoos, they're permanent. Sure, it's fun to see young people navigate the rollercoaster of life, but let's not slap a "temporary phase" sticker on everything. Today's avocado-toast-loving youngster might be tomorrow's avocado-toast-loving grandparent.

Meet Jason, a Millennial who found peace in yoga and meditation during college. Fast forward 40 years, and he's Grandpa Jason, and still starts each morning with a sun salutation, much to the amusement of his Gen Alpha grandkids.

So, instead of dismissing these quirks as youthful folly, middle-aged madness, or senior dementia, why not celebrate them as the enriching diversity they bring to our lives? Each generation's unique vibe is a chord in the grand symphony of human experience.

Susan, a Baby Boomer, adores her vinyl collection and won't let anyone touch her record player. Her granddaughter Lily, a Gen Z, respects this but convinces Susan to create a digital playlist with her, resulting in an afternoon of cross-generational bonding and music appreciation.

The young may bask in trending playlists while the older generation sways to timeless classics, but know that everyone's dancing to the tune of life's inescapable phases. Instead of waiting for someone to "outgrow" their passions or quirks, let's harmonize our generational vibes and create a timeless melody that we can all dance to.

By diving into the generational narratives, we see that while the stages of life may be universal, each generation adds its unique flavor, creating a multi-layered, enriching human experience. And isn't that something worth celebrating?

12. Complaints: Turn Common Complaints Into a Harmonious Workplace

In my workshops, people love to talk about what they dislike about other generations. Turns out that when it comes to grumbling about other generations, we're all world champions.

Seriously, if venting about other generations was an art, we'd all be Picassos! It's some people's favorite pastime to roast how way Gen Z can't read a paper map or how Baby Boomers still think Internet Explorer is 'cutting-edge.'

From Boomers accused of hoarding wealth to Gen Z being labeled as fun-seeking tech nerds, the stereotypes are as rampant as they are misleading.

Sometimes we default to seeing other generations as just obstacles. So we vent, and these can be a little bit funny when you put it all together. From that perspective...

- **Boomers are**, "Bossy jerks who take all the money, expected unearned obedience, care more about success than people, and force people to waste time in meetings and phone calls."
- **Gen X are**, "Pessimistic, antisocial, disrespectful rebels who always have to do things their own way."
- **Millennials are**, "Unrealistic, impatient, insecure, needy, disobedient, idealistic, snowflakes."
- **Gen Z are**, "Antisocial, progressive nerds who only care about having fun and being unique and spend more time hanging out than working."

An important note from the National Academy of Sciences Generational Labels project I participated in was that we don't really know for sure who Gen Z is and will become because of how long it takes to separate generational traits from age-related traits.

Imagine Bob, a Boomer who's an expert in mindfulness, sitting next to Tina, a Gen Z-er who's an ace at personal finance. Individual people's attributes often defy generational stereotypes, offering a rich canvas that no single label can capture.

We were still figuring out what made Millennials tick back in 2018, when they were in their "adulting" phase. And get this, buckle up, because Gen Z? Yeah, we won't have the full scoop on them until we're all zipping around in flying cars in 2037! I mean, I can barely predict what I'm having for lunch tomorrow, and here we are, trying to predict the future of generations.

Sarah, a Millennial, was an 'avocado toast' joke back in 2018. Today, she's a sustainability consultant who helps Fortune 500 companies reduce their carbon footprint. People evolve, and generational traits are no different.

But hey, don't let a little thing like not having all the facts stop us! We're gonna speculate, theorize, and probably make more unproven assumptions than a UFO convention. So, mark your calendars, folks, 'cause until 2037, we can go crazy wildly guessing and wildly disagreeing on who Gen Z really is!

But wait, there are more complaints! In my workshops, I consistently hear:

- **Boomers** are set in their ways, hate change, out of touch, hate technology, not culturally sensitive and have no filter on their mouths.
- **Gen X** gets called "Boomer Lite", is less creative than they think, also hate change, don't know how to say the right things and are overprotective.
- **Millennials** have too much screentime, are entitled, can't take constructive criticism, and question everything.
- **Gen Z** sometimes get called Millennials. Listen, old fogey, all young people are not Millennials! Gen Z is seen as anti-social, nerdy, disruptive, lazy, entitled, and too idealistic.

But we've been around the block long enough to know that saying someone's personality is all wrapped up in their birth year is about as accurate as predicting the weather by gazing into a crystal ball made of jellybeans.

So here's the secret sauce to world peace: *curiosity.* Yep, that's right. Instead of slapping labels on people like they're grocery store items, let's actually talk to them! Ask questions, spark conversations, and build connections like a professional Jenga stacker. Because the more we get to know each other, the more we'll realize that we're all just unique people trying to navigate life's weird obstacle course together.

So, what would happen if we approached each other with curiosity? What if we used our grievances as launching pads for constructive dialogue instead of finger-pointing?

Let's say John, a Boomer, asks his Gen Z intern, Lily, about her stance on work-life balance. Lily reciprocates by asking John what Abraham Lincoln was like in person- just kidding, she asks about his experiences during the early days of his career. This open exchange doesn't just eradicate labels; it creates understanding between generations.

The antidote to Generational Grumbling is not a silencing of opinions. Instead, it's the promotion of conversations that invite perspectives and deepen understanding.

In my workshops, attendees from all generations are given an "ice-breaker" assignment where they have to debunk a generational myth. The room buzzes with laughter and newfound appreciation, proving once again that understanding trumps stereotyping.

As we play this high-stakes game of generational Jenga, let's not forget that pulling out the wrong piece—a stereotype, a label—can topple our tower of understanding. But, with curiosity as our guide, we can build a structure that not only stands tall but celebrates the diverse pieces that make it whole.

With this perspective, we see that generational labels are not just limiting; they're opportunities lost. Opportunities to understand, connect, and thrive together in a world that is increasingly complex but wonderfully diverse. And isn't that something we should all aspire to?

13. Duality: Turn Generational Weaknesses Into Strengths

We've already seen some of the positive values and strengths of each generation, but we can also turn around every one of the preceding complaints to find generational strengths.

It's easy to misread each generation, but every cloud has a silver lining. When we pause to look at the strengths behind the stereotypes, an entirely different narrative emerges.

In workshops I give a few examples and then have the participants do the exercise themselves. Here's what I get back.

Boomers: Pillars of Wisdom and Consistency

They may be old, but that means they're experienced. Their perceived rigidity creates consistency. They may be out of touch with newer things but have a firm grasp on traditions, some of which are still useful. They may not be the biggest fans of technology, but that means more tech jobs for younger people. They may not always have a verbal filter, but you know they're being honest.

In every organization, there's value in experience and consistency. Imagine Susan, a Boomer who's not a tech wizard but who keeps the team grounded with her deep knowledge of industry standards and policies. Her experience is an asset, her consistency a virtue.

Gen X: Bridge-Builders and Problem Solvers

Gen X might be "Boomer Lite" but the Lite part is what they have in common with Millennials, which bridges the relationship. Even if Gen X is less creative than they think, they have reliable processes to create consistent success. They may be overprotective and pessimistic, but they are always looking for what could go wrong, and when it does, they're probably ready to fix it- and that creates safety, and quick recovery in emergencies.

Millennials: Innovators and Empathizers

Millennials may be on the Internet too much but they can find any info you need. They may seem entitled but that means they have high standards, and the courage to ask for what they need. Can't take criticism? Maybe it's because they have big, open hearts. Question everything? So do Gen X and Gen Z- and that's how we create innovation. Millennials drive the Information Age and bring emotional intelligence into workplaces.

Gen Z: Efficient Mavericks

Gen Z may seem nerdy, but they can solve your tech issues. They might look antisocial a times but they're also independent and resourceful, much like Gen X. What they do may be disruptive to some but actually initiates innovation. Labeled as lazy and entitled, Gen Z members are actually highly efficient and have a knack for questioning the status quo—traits essential for innovation.

The Art of Strength-Spotting

In my workshops, the exercise of flipping complaints to compliments unveils a treasure trove of generational strengths.

Participants in my workshops have realized that their "rigid" Boomer colleague is actually a valuable mentor. Or that the "impatient" Millennial coworker is a catalyst for much-needed change.

So, next time you catch yourself or someone else making a sweeping generational generalization, pause and consider the underlying strengths

Example: Your next team project could benefit from the combined strengths of Lisa's (Boomer) experience, Tom's (Gen X) risk assessment, Jenny's (Millennial) tech-savviness, and Tim's (Gen Z) efficiency.

By shifting the lens through which we view each generation, we can evolve from a culture of stereotyping to a culture of strength-spotting. This transformation will not only enrich our individual lives but also turn our organizations into vibrant, multi-generational collages of talent and innovation.

Generational Turnover and Team Dynamics

14. Melting Pot: Succeed in Business by Leveraging Multi-Generational Synergy

Some leaders see only the strengths of their older employees and the problems with younger ones. Why is this? Each group has somewhat different values.

It's tempting for some of these leaders to try to run their company mainly through older generations. They hope the younger ones will get real, or shape up.

In fact, this type of leader is a Blocker or Limper (from the "Catalysts" chapter) whose companies are going to die of old age. The truth is: we need everybody.

If you think clinging to a single generational tribe is the key to running a successful business, think again. Today, more than ever, our businesses need a symphony of generational talents to not just survive, but thrive.

Some leaders might think the younger generation is a riddle too complex to solve and might want to exclusively focus on older, more familiar talents. But that's a mistake.

Imagine a tech startup full of Gen Z and Millennials but devoid of Boomer and Gen X wisdom. When a crisis hits that needs deep industry knowledge, where is the wisdom and experience? Or conversely, a traditional enterprise teeming with Boomers but lacking fresh blood will suffer from a perilous stagnation, and most likely, a growing misunderstanding of the marketplace.

If you've mostly worked with people like yourself, it may be a new idea that more diverse teams can be stronger teams. But it shouldn't be strange- we already know that companies need people with very different skills like sales, marketing, operations, accounting, and so on. Every criticism we have of other generations contains a corresponding strength.

People who seem "different" also have different strengths. And when you all work together, you work better. You pull together more resources and abilities. Your organization grows in its capabilities and breadth.

It's time to debunk the myth that uniformity means strength. The following are some transformative benefits when multiple generations harmonize in a business setting.

You share knowledge. Each generation brings unique skills, experiences, and perspectives. Collaborating across generations allows for the exchange of knowledge, best practices, and lessons learned, fostering a more knowledgeable and well-rounded workforce. A team that encourages generational mingling becomes a university unto itself. Boomers' lifetime of wisdom meets the digital prowess of Gen Z, creating a self-sustaining cycle of growth.

You get enhanced creativity and innovation. Different generations often approach problem-solving and decision-making in different ways. By working together, teams can leverage this diversity of thought, leading to increased creativity and innovation in finding solutions and developing new ideas. Different generations have unique problem-solving styles. When these worlds collide, expect a burst of creativity that could be the next game-changer.

Productivity improves. A harmonious multi-generational workforce can lead to enhanced productivity and efficiency. Each generation can capitalize on its strengths, complement each other's weaknesses, and drive better overall performance. A multi-generational workforce can be an assembly line of productivity where each generation adds a piece of excellence to the final product.

Communication Skills are enhanced. Interacting with colleagues from different age groups can improve communication skills as individuals must adapt their communication styles to ensure mutual understanding and respect. The diversity of age within a team becomes a workshop for improving communication. How you talk to a Boomer will sharpen how you communicate with a Gen Z, and vice versa.

Employee engagement and retention goes up. A work environment that values and respects the contributions of all generations fosters higher employee engagement and satisfaction. It also contributes to better retention rates as employees feel appreciated and included. Employees tend to stick around when they feel valued and understood. Inter-generational acceptance is a big morale booster.

You have access to more talent. Embracing a multi-generational approach to hiring means that a company can draw from a wider talent pool. This can lead to hiring individuals with diverse backgrounds, skills, and experiences, enhancing the organization's capabilities. Imagine the diversity of skill sets and experiences you'd miss out on by sticking to one age group. Multi-generational hiring is like having your pick of the best crops from different fields.

Your corporate culture becomes more positive. Encouraging intergenerational collaboration can contribute to a positive and inclusive company culture. When employees feel valued and respected, they're more likely to be motivated, loyal, and enthusiastic about their work. A culture of inter-generational respect can turn your organization into a sanctuary where employees don't just earn but also learn and grow.

You can adapt to changing markets. Different generations have varying needs and preferences as consumers. Having a diverse workforce allows a company to better understand and connect with these diverse market segments. A multi-generational team is like having a built-in focus group for market research.

There are more learning and growth opportunities. Millennials can tap into the Boomers' wealth of experience, while Boomers can get a quick lesson on the latest tech trends from Gen Z. It's mutual mentorship in action.

Succession planning is easier. When generations work in synergy, the transition of leadership roles becomes a non-event instead of a disruptive change. Encouraging knowledge transfer and mentorship between generations helps ensure a smooth succession planning process as older employees retire and younger ones take on more significant roles.

Overall, fostering a collaborative and inclusive environment that values the strengths of multiple generations can lead to improved teamwork, higher job satisfaction, better business outcomes, and a more sustainable and adaptable organization.

If you find yourself resistant to multi-generational collaboration, it might be time for some introspection.

Jane, a Gen X department manager, realized that her resistance to hiring Millennials was affecting her team's creativity. After embracing a multi-generational approach, her department became the most innovative unit in the company.

So, let's rewrite the narrative from one that points out generational flaws to one that celebrates generational strengths. That's the only way we can pave the road to a more inclusive, effective, and future-proof business landscape.

In a world where adaptability is key, a multi-generational workforce is not just a luxury; it's a necessity. By leveraging the unique strengths of each generation, companies can build stronger, more resilient organizations.

15. Synergize! Boost Productivity Through Effective Team Dynamics

In a world as complex and fast-changing as ours, the concept of 'us vs. them' is a recipe for stagnation. However, when we view our differences as an ecosystem of strengths, we discover the secret to unparalleled success. When old meets new, great things happen.

You may believe one leader can do it all, but even Superman had his Kryptonite and ultimately needed a Justice League to survive and win.

Consider Bob, a Boomer CEO who thought he could navigate the digital marketing world alone. It was only after failing to generate online traction that he admitted he needed the Gen Z tech whizzes.

One benefit of valuing everyone despite their differences is that they have different strengths from you.

Let's break down the multifaceted benefits of valuing everyone for their unique abilities:

- **Tech-Savvy Millennials:** Hate technology? No problem! The younger generation can be your IT wizards, transforming your digital dread into a functioning asset.
- **The Hunger for Change:** Feeling too settled in your ways? Younger colleagues are not just receptive to change; they are catalysts for innovation.
- **A Two-Way Mentorship Street:** While younger generations may lack certain life and career experiences, they're often eager to learn if approached the right way. Mentorship is a two-way street: your wisdom for their fresh perspective.
- **The Pursuit of Balance:** Struggling with work-life equilibrium? Millennials and Gen Z can be your personal gurus in finding that elusive balance. They'll help you align idealism with reality, but you have to be willing to listen.

So, how do we unlock this treasure trove of generational harmony?

- **Start with Communication:** The first step is often as simple as initiating an open dialogue. Be the leader who invites conversation rather than shutting it down.
- **Sprinkle in Respect:** Without mutual respect, even the best ideas will fall on deaf ears. Respect is the foundation upon which trust is built.
- **Seal it with Trust:** Open-mindedness fosters trust. Without trust, mentorship becomes dictatorship, and cooperation turns into coercion.

Here's a hypothetical Example: Emily, a Gen X manager, found herself overwhelmed by the new software. Initially reluctant, she finally allowed her younger team members to take the reins. Not only did productivity skyrocket, but she also found time to impart her negotiation skills to her millennial counterparts.

It's high time we debunk the notion that valuing differences is a zero-sum game. It's not about losing your identity; it's about creating a fabric where each thread contributes to a stronger, more beautiful whole.

The core message is clear: the confluence of generational talents, orchestrated through communication, respect, and trust, can become the ultimate competitive advantage for any organization. So, are you ready to embrace the full spectrum of strengths that generational diversity brings?

16. Pioneers: Capitalize on the Coming Workforce Evolution with Gen Z

"The times, they are changing," as Bob Dylan sang. As the winds of transformation blow, they carry with them the names of the Gen Z workforce. (Along with a few "idiot winds," or generational grumbling.)

Trying to fit Gen Z into a traditional workplace is like trying to fit a square peg into a round hole. But it's not them that needs changing; it's the hole.

Can we afford to ignore the seismic shifts brought about by Gen Z? First and foremost, leaders must appreciate the unique qualities that Gen Z brings to the table. Denying or resisting these changes will not only harm your organization's culture but will also lead to issues in staffing, turnover, and productivity. Think of this as a turning point; embrace it as an opportunity rather than viewing it as a threat. For leaders who adapt, the rewards in employee loyalty and performance can be immense.

Consider the case of Jenny, a CEO who took the time to understand that her Gen Z employees favored a more flexible work environment. She adapted her company policies to incorporate remote work options and flexible hours. As a result, employee satisfaction levels surged, especially among Gen Z staff, who felt respected and understood.

Why risk obsolescence by clinging to outdated values? Failure to address value misalignment in an organization can undermine even the best teams. A strong set of core values that adapt to generational shifts is the bedrock of a successful organization. In an ever-changing market, those who resist change risk obsolescence.

Mike, a COO, understood that his company's long-standing value of "time in the office equals productivity" was outdated. After conducting a staff survey, he launched new metrics focused on project completion and quality, aligning better with Gen Z's values of efficiency and outcome-based performance.

Are you ready to meet Gen Z's unique financial challenges head-on? The economics that Gen Z faces are vastly different from those of previous generations. Understand this and be part of the solution. Proactively adjusting compensation structures can be a strong statement that you value and respect what they bring to the table. This leads to longer-term commitment and reduced turnover.

Emily, the HR Director of a marketing firm, introduced a "graduated compensation" program. This allowed younger employees to earn additional income through company-sponsored training programs, thereby addressing their need for financial security and growth.

What's the price of not offering a clear career path in today's transient work landscape? The career landscape has changed; gone are the days of pensions and lifetime employment with a single company. Leaders must communicate a vision of a rewarding career trajectory for their employees to ensure mutual loyalty. Be transparent and true to your word; otherwise, expect your human capital to move to greener pastures.

Steven, a middle manager, sat down individually with his team members to discuss their 5-year career paths within the organization. By outlining growth opportunities and setting mutual expectations, he saw an increase in team loyalty and productivity.

How can we forge a meaningful connection in a digital world? Engagement isn't just about salaries or job titles. Effective communication, the art of motivation, and genuine empathy play equally critical roles. Leaders must not only be skilled in traditional managerial functions but also be adept at leveraging technology for remote work and virtual engagement.

Lisa, a department head, introduced a "Virtual Coffee Break" using video conferencing tools. This provided a platform for remote workers to socialize and share ideas, replicating the social aspects of an office environment and making everyone, including Gen Z workers, feel included and engaged.

The Research

Here are seven science-backed recommendations for working with Generation Z employees:

- Open up to modern means of communication[1].
- Value skills that are important to Gen Z'ers[2].

- Create a mentoring program with Millennial and Gen X employees to bridge across generations and to boost meaningful collaboration across age cohorts[3].
- Create a peer or buddy program where you pair Gen Z team members together so that they always have someone to contact for support[3].
- Provide fair wages and partner treatment[4].
- Clearly communicate essential job responsibilities, expectations for hours worked, travel, and working conditions[5].
- Provide opportunities for professional development and growth[6].

References

1. Expectations of Generation Z - A Challenge for Academic Didactic Staff. (n.d.). ERIC.
2. Reaching and Retaining the Next Generation: Adapting to the Expectations of Gen Z in the Classroom. (n.d.). ERIC.
3. Helping Gen Z Employees Find Their Place at Work. (2023, January 18). Harvard Business
4. Dobrowolski, Z., Drozdowski, G., & Panait, M. (2022). Understanding the Impact of Generation Z on Risk Management—A Preliminary Views on Values, Competencies, and Ethics of the Generation Z in Public Administration. International Journal of Environmental Research and Public Health, 19(7), 3868.
5. Schroth, H. A. (2019). Are You Ready for Gen Z in the Workplace? California Management Review, 61(3), 5–23.
6. Generation Z in the Workplace through the Lenses of Human Resource Professionals – A Qualitative Study. (n.d.). ResearchGate.

Part III: Aligning Corporate and Individual Values

17. Aligned Values: The Foundation For Success or Failure

Why do we so often misunderstand the term "values"? It's a concept laden with complexity, yet its core message is simple and universal. Values aren't just moral high grounds or a singular worldview. They are the compass that guides us, the North Star in a sky filled with countless distractions.

Can we truly navigate the turbulent seas of life without recognizing what our compass is pointing toward?

Your values define what matters most to you, and acknowledging them isn't a sign of rigidity but an emblem of self-awareness. They serve as the gravitational force that keeps your world intact amidst chaos.

Think of your values as the roots that ground you, providing nourishment and stability. Just as a mighty oak stands tall because of its deeply embedded roots, you too can rise above challenges when you're anchored by your values.

Here are some examples of the kinds of one-word values I'm talking about:

Personal Values: Empathy, Integrity, Resilience, Compassion, Authenticity, Humility, Accountability, Curiosity, Patience, Ambition, Creativity, Determination, Flexibility, Gratitude, Loyalty, Optimism, Perseverance, Adaptability, Empowerment, Kindness, Open-mindedness, Trustworthiness, Courage, Generosity, Responsibility, Self-discipline, Self-awareness, Teamwork, Balance, Independence, Wisdom, Collaboration, Positivity, Honesty, Innovation, Accountability, Respect, Self-motivation, Authenticity, Accountability, Empowerment, Adaptability, Tenacity, Patience, Tolerance, Purposefulness, Integrity, Synergy, Excellence, and Harmony.

Corporate Values: Customer-Centric, Sustainability, Innovation, Quality, Ethics, Diversity, Efficiency, Transparency, Collaboration, Leadership, Agility, Accountability, Excellence, Empowerment, Trust, Integrity, Resilience, Flexibility, Openness, Creativity, Teamwork, Customer-Focused, Adaptability, Social Responsibility, Customer Satisfaction, Reliability, Continuous Improvement, Community Involvement, Empathy, Environmental Stewardship, Inclusivity, Global Perspective, Technological Advancement, Sustainability, Ethical Practices, Employee Development, Customer Loyalty, Profitability, Positive Impact, Open Communication, Problem Solving, Efficiency, Learning Culture, Honesty, Social Impact, Workplace Safety, Quality Assurance, Adaptation, Financial Integrity, and Growth.

The Research

7 research findings about corporate values in workplaces:

- A psychologically healthy workplace is essential for employee well-being and productivity12.
- Companies that foster psychologically healthy workplaces are more likely to retain employees3.
- Feeling valued at work is linked to better physical and mental health, as well as higher levels of engagement, satisfaction, and motivation4.

- Workplace spirituality, including personal, organizational, and interactive values, can impact employee outcomes5.
- A sense of belonging and social support in the workplace can lead to happier, healthier, and more productive employees6.
- Companies that prioritize worker voice and equity have more positive workplace cultures1.
- Positive workplace practices, such as employee recognition, work-life balance, and opportunities for growth and development, can improve employee retention and satisfaction2.

References

1. American Psychological Association. (2023). 2023 Work in America Survey: Workplaces as engines of psychological health and well-being.
2. American Psychological Association. (n.d.). The Psychologically Healthy Workplace: Building a Win-Win Environment for Organizations and Employees.
3. American Psychological Association. (2006, March 6). Employees: A company's best asset.
4. American Psychological Association. (2012, March 8). APA survey finds feeling valued at work linked to well-being and performance.
5. Kostere, K., & Pearsall, M. J. (2007). Workplace values and outcomes: Exploring personal, organizational, and interactive workplace spirituality. Journal of Business and Psychology, 22(3), 265-278.
6. American Psychological Association. (2023, July 13). A sense of belonging is crucial for employees. How employers can foster connection and social support.

18. Harmony: Build a Cohesive, Engaged Workforce Through Aligned Values

When your values conflict with someone else's, it's easy to have arguments and misunderstandings.

When we judge other people for having different values than us, we shut the door on relationship, collaboration, and teamwork.

Is a team really a team if its values are at war? Picture this: Marketing thirsts for groundbreaking innovations to amplify impact. On the other side, IT raises the shield of security, warning that new could mean risky. The result? A gridlock of frustration. What you have is a ship where the crew pulls in opposite directions. Will that ship sail or sink?

Imagine a project where Marketing insists on implementing an AI chatbot for customer support, citing efficiency and customer engagement. IT, however, sees this as a Pandora's box of data privacy issues. Conflict escalates, deadlines are missed, and neither department can claim victory.

Do you want to lead a fractured team or a symphony where each section plays its part? To move forward in harmony, we must first stand on common ground. The team that sings from the same song sheet will naturally outperform discordant competitors.

Take the story of Sarah, a visionary leader who recognized these tensions. She orchestrated a "Values Summit" where each department presented its core values and then found the overlapping themes. This became the shared compass, guiding all decision-making henceforth.

But let's confront the elephant in the room: Why do so many organizations falter in their values?

- **Ignored Values:** Do your employees even know what the company values are? Values that collect dust on a website are as useful as a compass locked in a treasure chest.
- **Inconsistent Values:** Words without action are mere illusions. How can employees feel anchored if

the leadership's actions drift away from the stated values?

- **Top-Down Dictatorship:** Can values dictated from the mountaintop ever resonate in the valley? True commitment comes when everyone has a say. Don't be potato.
- **Irrelevant Values:** If your values are not your playbook for decision-making, then what are they? Ornamental trinkets?
- **Outdated Values:** Could yesterday's wisdom be today's folly? Adaptation is the name of the survival game.

What monster is born when values are ignored or mismatched? A house divided against itself, full of silos, self-interest, and internal warfare. It's a scene where everyone becomes a general but there's no army.

Can such a place ever attract and retain talent, let alone customers?

We have to get on the same page with values if we all want to go in the same direction. The team or organization that does this is going to get further than those who never resolve their conflict and figure out how to support each other.

The Research

Findings about aligned or misaligned values in workplaces:

- Misalignment in leader and follower perceptions of leader-member exchange (LMX) can negatively affect employee innovative performance[1].
- Organizational cultures that are not aligned with group fault lines can negatively impact performance[2].
- Cultural alignment and congruence between organizational and individual values can lead to increased employee engagement and patient satisfaction in healthcare organizations[3].

- Perceived stress management should be aligned with organizational cultures and employee competencies to reduce employee stress[4].
- Employee-workplace alignment theory suggests that alignment between people and the office environment can lead to increased job satisfaction and productivity[5].
- Misalignment between employees' perceptions of organizational and supervisor unfairness can lead to destructive voice responses[6].
- Misalignment between individual and institutional values can lead to a lack of faculty satisfaction and retention in academic medicine[3].

References

1. https://www.researchgate.net/publication/340788317_Two_to_Tango_Implications_of_Alignment_and_Misalignment_in_Leader_and_Follower_Perceptions_of_LMX
2. https://psycnet.apa.org/record/2011-14076-001
3. https://www.ncbi.nlm.nih.gov/pmc/articles/PMC7010974/
4. https://www.ncbi.nlm.nih.gov/pmc/articles/PMC9032235/
5. https://research.tudelft.nl/files/141731334/10.1201_9781003128830_23_chapterpdf.pdf
6. https://journals.sagepub.com/doi/10.1177/10596011221074155?icid=int.sj-abstract.citing-articles.692

19. Core: The Common Ground that Transcends Generational Barriers

Let's address a popular myth: that generations are isolated islands in a sea of time, each floating away from the other. This couldn't be further from the truth. Sure, each generation has its own set of trends, cultural shifts, and yes, questionable fashion choices. But should we let bell-bottoms, flannel shirts, or skinny jeans define us?

Imagine a family dinner where a Boomer, a Millennial, and a Gen Z'er are present. Despite the age differences, all express a shared joy for a stable home and the chance to influence positive change in society. So why is there still a disconnect?

We often focus on what sets us apart, but it's the common values that build bridges:

- **Boomers and Millennials:** the optimists, envisioning a future better than today.
- **Boomers and Gen Z:** the fortresses of stability in an ever-changing world.
- **Gen X, Millennials, and Gen Z:** the rebels and the balancers, striving for work-life equilibrium while questioning the status quo.

Specifically, Millennials and Gen Z are the torchbearers of social progress and champions of diversity. And let's not forget, they also crave coaching and mentorship, albeit with Gen Z's more independent, DIY approach.

So, what are the golden threads that weave through the generations? From the boardrooms to the classrooms, I've found that these seven values resonate:

- **Feeling Respected:** Isn't respect the very cornerstone of human interaction?
- **Being Listened to:** Who doesn't want their voice to be heard in a cacophony of opinions?
- **Opportunities for Mentoring:** Wouldn't you agree that a guide can sometimes show us shortcuts to wisdom?

- **Understanding the Big Picture:** Doesn't everyone want to be part of something larger than themselves?
- **Effective Communication:** Isn't dialogue the key to unlocking mutual understanding?
- **Positive Feedback:** Don't we all bloom a little brighter under the sunshine of affirmation?
- **Exchange of Ideas:** Wouldn't you say that fresh ideas are the oxygen that keeps a community alive?

Is there anyone out there who would willingly opt out of any of these values? I have posed this question countless times to diverse crowds and have yet to hear a single 'yes.'

So, if we were to crystallize these values into a single-word lexicon, we'd have:

- **Respect:** The currency that never devalues.
- **Listening:** The silent symphony of empathy.
- **Mentoring:** The ancestral passing of wisdom.
- **Planning:** The map for a communal journey.
- **Communication:** The bridge between isolated islands.
- **Affirmation:** The nectar of self-worth.
- **Conversation:** The heartbeat of civilization.

Questions to Consider

- Have you ever felt a conflict of values with someone from another generation? How did you navigate it?
- Are you actively contributing to a culture of shared values where you work or live? If not, what's holding you back?
- Could aligning these universal values be the key to unlocking the generational potential within us all?

So, as you contemplate these actions and questions, remember that bridging the generational divide is not a pipe dream—it's a tangible goal that begins with recognizing the common threads that bind us all. By putting these values into action, we lay the cornerstone for a more harmonious, productive, and meaningful co-existence across all ages.

The Research

Based on research, here are five findings about work-related values that all generations share:

- Work values associated with sustainable organizational development or basic needs are highly similar across generations[2].
- All generations value work outcomes, craftsmanship, and the moral importance of work[5].
- All generations place importance on the work itself, as well as the opportunity for personal growth and development[1].
- All generations value work-life balance and flexibility in the workplace[6].
- All generations value job security and stability[3].

References

1. Hansen, J.-I. C., & Leuty, M. E. (2012). Work values across generations. Journal of Career Assessment, 20(1), 34-52.
2. Lyons, S. T., & Kuron, L. K. (2014). Generational differences in work-related attitudes: A meta-analysis. Journal of Business and Psychology, 29(2), 169-184.
3. Parry, E., & Urwin, P. (2011). Generational differences in work values: A review of theory and evidence. International Journal of Management Reviews, 13(1), 79-96.
4. Smola, K. W., & Sutton, C. D. (2002). Generational differences: Revisiting generational work values for

the new millennium. Journal of Organizational Behavior, 23(4), 363-382.

5. Mencl, J., & Lester, S. W. (2014). More alike than different: What generations value and how the values affect employee workplace perceptions. Journal of Leadership, Accountability and Ethics, 11(4), 1-12.

6. Rudolph, C. W., & Zacher, H. (2015). Intergenerational perceptions and conflicts in multiage and multigenerational work environments. In Facing the Challenges of a Multi-Age Workforce: A Use-Inspired Approach (pp. 253-282). Routledge.

20. Obstacles: Navigate Differences to Improve Organization-Wide Efficiency

Every organization is a melting pot of different values, priorities, and appetites for change. It's like an orchestra where every instrument—each with its own timbre, range, and role—must harmonize to create a symphony. The question is, how can you be the conductor who brings it all together?

Within any organization, you'll find individuals who are passionate about improvement and innovation, as well as those who are resistant to change. These value differences manifest not only at an individual level but also at a departmental level. This clash of values can create friction, inefficiency, and sometimes, a culture of stagnation.

Let's explore some hypothetical scenarios that demonstrate these departmental conflicts: Also, there are departments and job descriptions that naturally have different values. Here are three scenarios and how to resolve them.

Marketing vs IT

Marketing may be laser-focused on driving growth, pushing to integrate the latest tech solutions for customer engagement. On the other hand, IT—tasked with maintaining security protocols—may flag these initiatives as high-risk.

Rather than dismissing IT as naysayers, turn them into collaborators. Set a problem-solving deadline and encourage IT to work with Marketing to find a secure yet effective solution. This approach promotes both departments' values: innovation for Marketing and security for IT.

Project Team vs Accounting & Legal

Your project team needs to expedite a vendor contract to meet project milestones. But the accounting and legal departments have processes that could delay project kick-off.

Communication is key. Make accounting and legal part of the conversation early on. Make them aware of the project timeline and the importance of meeting deadlines. Better yet, hold them accountable for these deadlines, just as you would any other department.

HR vs Generational Needs

Suppose your HR department is steeped in traditional methods that don't resonate with younger employees.

Engage HR in a brainstorming session focused on Millennial and Gen Z needs. Introduce them to current trends and training programs. Set measurable goals, such as specific demographic targets or turnover rate reductions, to instill a sense of urgency and purpose.

It's your job as a leader to guide these departments on how they can work together successfully. Sometimes that guidance requires getting into the weeds and getting quite specific. Often the solution requires compromise. Make sure they know that compromise is not a bad word- in fact, compromise is the foundation of collaboration.

As a leader, your role is to be the mediator, the interpreter, and sometimes the judge. You must dive deep into these value conflicts and facilitate solutions that everyone can buy into. Compromise isn't a sign of weakness or indecisiveness; it's the bedrock of collaboration and improvement.

Action Steps

1. Conduct a departmental "Values Mapping" session to identify the core values driving each department's decision-making process.
2. Establish inter-departmental "Collaborative Councils" to work on specific challenges, incorporating diverse values to find the best solutions.
3. Use metrics to monitor how well values are being aligned with outcomes. For instance, track how quickly IT solutions are implemented post-approval,

or measure the engagement levels in different age groups within the company.

Reflection Questions

Are there value-based conflicts in your organization that you have yet to address? What are the perceived barriers?

Have you, as a leader, been hesitant to mediate value conflicts? If so, why?

What department in your organization is most aligned with its core values, and why do you think that is?

Is your role as a leader to enforce a set of monolithic organizational values, or is it to synthesize a multitude of departmental and individual values into a coherent, but adaptable, framework for success?

So as you navigate your role as a leader, consider that your task isn't to erase these value differences, but to harmonize them into a beautiful, cohesive melody that is your organization's culture.

The Research

Here are five recommendations for dealing with value-conflicts at work:

- Provide training in conflict resolution skills[1]. Research shows that such training can lead to improved teamwork, productivity, and employee satisfaction.
- Treat people with equality and respect[2]. This applies to all interactions, whether with peers or not.
- Use a values conflict resolution assessment[3]. This tool can help identify areas of conflict and guide resolution efforts.
- Address value conflicts between clients and clinicians using a model that emphasizes mutual respect and collaboration[4].
- Be aware of your own values, attitudes, beliefs, and behaviors, and avoid imposing values that are inconsistent with counseling goals[5].

References

1. Conflict Management: Difficult Conversations with Difficult People. (n.d.). PMC.
2. Ten Simple Rules for avoiding and resolving conflicts with your colleagues. (2019). PMC.
3. Development of a Values Conflict Resolution Assessment. (1987). APA PsycNet.
4. Farnsworth, J. K., & Callahan, J. L. (2013). A model for addressing client–clinician value conflict. APA PsycNet.
5. When Values and Ethics Conflict: The Counselor's Role and Responsibility. (2012). ERIC.

21. Rebirth: Revamp Your Culture for Better Retention

In a rapidly evolving business landscape, corporate values aren't just fancy taglines to display on your website or office walls. They are the linchpins that anchor your organizational culture, shape your brand, and influence both employee retention and productivity. So how do you update these values in a way that speaks to multiple generations, diverse cultural backgrounds, and varying departmental interests?

Whether your team comprises Baby Boomers nostalgic for the "good old days," or Gen Z'ers eager for transformative change, it's crucial to form a unified set of corporate values. This unity won't just prevent workplace discord; it can significantly uplift your overall organizational health.

Here is an inclusive process to get everyone on the same page:

1. **Announce the Initiative:** Transparency is essential. Inform everyone—across all levels—that the company is embarking on an exercise to revisit and update its core values.

2. **Self-Discovery Exercise:** Assign everyone the task of identifying their own core values. This gives employees ownership of the process and makes them more likely to buy into the final set.

3. **Customer Insights:** Use a survey or other methods to glean what values your customers prize most in your industry and from you as a provider.

4. **Leadership Alignment:** Convene a meeting of your top executives and managers to review and consolidate the values identified by employees, leadership, and customers. Prioritize them based on strategic objectives and broader company goals.

5. **Collective Feedback:** Hold an all-hands meeting to present what the leadership has synthesized. Use this meeting as a platform for open discussion and feedback.

6. **Final Integration:** Take everyone's input into account and have another leadership meeting to finalize these values.

7. **Communication:** Once the values are finalized, disseminate this information to your entire workforce and customer base. Use multiple channels—emails, internal newsletters, and customer bulletins—to ensure the message is received far and wide.

After establishing your updated values, embed them into your everyday operations and decision-making processes. Tie performance metrics to these values to create a coherent, value-driven organization.

Action Steps

- Create onboarding materials that reflect the new values to ensure new hires are immediately aligned.
- Review and revise, if necessary, your reward and recognition systems to celebrate value-aligned behavior.
- Periodically revisit these values to ensure they remain relevant as both the external market and internal dynamics evolve.

Reflective Questions

- How will you measure the impact of these updated values on employee retention and productivity?
- Is your leadership team consistently embodying these new values?
- How can you involve your customer base in the value alignment process moving forward?

Updating your corporate values isn't just a "feel-good" activity; it's a strategic move. As a leader, you're tasked with the vital role of guiding this transformation. By creating an inclusive process and continually aligning operations with these updated values, you're laying the groundwork for a cohesive, effective, and enduring organization.

How to Let Everybody Know What's Happening

In any transformational initiative, transparent and effective communication is the cornerstone. Just sending out an email isn't enough; the message should resonate, excite, and prepare your team for the journey ahead. How do you announce an update to corporate values that not only informs but also engages?

Your announcement can be framed in a way that leverages storytelling, transparency, and inclusivity.

- **Storytelling:** Start by giving context. Explain what prompted this change. Whether it's industry shifts or internal developments, a story adds weight and understanding to the initiative.
- **Transparency:** Make sure everyone understands this isn't a top-down approach. Clearly state how every voice in the company will be heard in this process.
- **Inclusivity:** Mention that this effort extends beyond employees and includes customer perspectives as well, making it an all-encompassing value system.

Give them a heads up. It could be an email as simple as:

Subject Line: New Corporate Values That Will Involve and Help Everyone

Hey team!

We're going to be updating our corporate values soon so that we can make the best decisions for you and for customers, and be sure we're all on the same page about priorities.

This values update will be a process, and we'll be getting everyone involved. This is about knowing what everyone thinks is important, including customers, employees, and leadership.

The goal is to create a prioritized values list that will help us make great decisions and keep everybody as happy as possible. It should be a fun process- no, really!

More info to follow.

[Your sign-off]

Or it could be more in-depth like this:

Subject Line: Embarking on a Journey to Refresh Our Core Values

Dear [Team/Company Name],

Exciting news! We're about to embark on a journey to reevaluate and update our corporate values. With seismic shifts in our industry and societal values, this is the perfect time to ensure that our guiding principles align with what's important to each of us, as well as to our valued customers.

Here's what's going to happen:

1. Discovery Phase: Over the next week, we'll be providing you with some tools and exercises to help you identify what values resonate with you personally.

2. Customer Insights: We're also taking this opportunity to find out what our customers value most about our services.

3. Collaborative Synthesis: Through a series of focused discussions, your managers and leadership will work to merge these diverse perspectives into a cohesive values list.

The aim? To establish a set of core values that will guide our decisions, prioritize our objectives, and foster an environment where everyone is aligned and engaged.

Details about each phase will follow, but rest assured, this is a collective effort and your input is invaluable. Together, we'll shape a vibrant and effective culture that benefits us all.

Best regards,
[Your Name]
[Your Position]

Reflective Questions

- What platforms are most effective for your organization's internal communications?

- How will you ensure that the message is accessible to everyone, including remote workers and various departments?

The goal isn't just to inform but to invite dialogue and participation. An effective announcement sets the tone for a successful values update, turning a corporate initiative into a collective journey.

How and Why to Help Employees Discover Their Personal Values

Understanding personal values is the first step towards creating a harmonious and high-performing workplace. It allows for more authentic conversations and provides a baseline for what truly matters to everyone. But how do you encourage employees to embark on this introspective journey?

Let's start with a clear understanding of why personal values are indispensable:

- **Understanding:** Identifying personal values fosters a climate of respect and understanding among team members.
- **Alignment:** People are more likely to stay where they feel their personal values align with their professional environment.
- **Engagement:** Employees who see a connection between their personal values and their work are likely to be more engaged and motivated.

Step-by-Step Guide to Facilitating Personal Value Discovery

1. **Leadership Paves the Way:** Before rolling it out to everyone, leaders should first explore their personal values. This sets an example and allows leaders to guide the process more effectively.
2. **Provide Robust Tools:** The internet is teeming with personal value assessment tools. One highly recommended platform is personalvalu.es. These

tools offer a structured way to explore what matters most to an individual.

3. **Walk Through the Process:** Host a virtual or in-person seminar explaining how to use these tools and what to expect from the process. You could invite a professional facilitator or an HR representative well-versed in personal development to lead this.

4. **Time & Space:** Encourage employees to take time out of their workday to engage with these tools. This indicates that the organization values this process.

5. **Open Dialogue:** Once everyone has had a chance to explore their personal values, organize team meetings where they can share their discoveries if they wish. This sharing can be powerful in building team cohesion.

6. **Integrate with Corporate Values:** Explain that the aim is not to replace but to align corporate values with personal ones, for a more integrated approach to work and life.

Considerations for Implementation

- **Privacy:** Assure employees that their individual results are their own and won't be used for any kind of performance assessment.
- **Accessibility:** Ensure that all tools and processes are accessible to remote or differently-abled employees.
- **Ongoing Support:** Provide resources for deeper exploration into personal values and how they connect with career development.

Questions for Reflection

- How will you measure the impact of this personal value discovery process on employee satisfaction and engagement?
- What mechanisms can you put in place to ensure that these personal values are respected and integrated into team dynamics?

Discovering personal values is not just a "nice-to-have" activity but a critical exercise that can significantly influence workplace culture, employee engagement, and ultimately, business success.

How to Conduct a Values-Based Customer Survey

Understanding the values that matter to your customers can profoundly affect your business—shaping everything from product development to marketing strategies. Conducting a customer survey focused on values is an effective way to get these crucial insights. Below, you'll find a comprehensive guide to help you achieve just that.

Before diving into the "how," let's examine why knowing customer values is essential:

- **Tailored Offerings:** Understanding customer values helps you craft products and services that resonate with their needs.
- **Targeted Marketing:** A deep grasp of values allows you to develop marketing campaigns that speak directly to customer priorities.
- **Customer Retention:** When customers feel their values align with yours, they're more likely to stay loyal to your brand.

The Nuts and Bolts of Setting Up a Customer Survey

- **Choose the Right Tool:** Whether you opt for SurveyMonkey, Google Forms, or a specialized customer experience platform, the tool should be user-friendly and allow easy data analysis.

- **Design the Survey:** Open-ended questions are a potent way to dig deep into customer values without leading them into predetermined answers. This helps in drawing out more authentic responses.

Sample Questions to Ask in Your Survey

- What values matter most to you when choosing a company like ours?
- Could you list your top three corporate values?
- What values do you appreciate in our brand?
- What motivated you to choose us initially?
- Why have you remained a customer?

Adapt the questions according to the type of product or service you provide. Moreover, consider segmenting your customer base and tailoring the survey to different segments for more precise insights.

Especially in B2B contexts, it may be beneficial to collect data from multiple individuals within the client company to gain a rounded perspective.

Data Interpretation and Next Steps

- **Data Aggregation:** Compile all the responses into a centralized data platform for easier analysis.
- **Value Identification:** Translate the responses into one-word values. For instance, if someone mentions "trustworthy service," you might categorize this under "Trust."
- **Pattern Recognition:** Identify recurring values to understand common trends among your customer base. These insights will help tailor your corporate values in alignment with customer expectations.

Questions for Reflection

- How do you plan to integrate these customer values into your product development and marketing strategies?

- What mechanisms can you put in place to regularly update this values data?

Understanding your customers' values isn't a one-time event but an ongoing process that can provide invaluable insights into your market positioning and how you can meet or exceed customer expectations.

Helping Leaders Lead the Values Update

In a rapidly changing business landscape, aligning corporate values across leadership is vital for consistent decision-making and fostering a unified organizational culture. Here's a detailed guide on how to effectively lead a values update meeting with your company's leaders.

What you need here is a meeting. Possibly several.

Who's in the meeting? How you define the "leaders" here is up to you. It's going to depend on your company size and structure. I would keep it to 20 max, though, to ensure everyone can contribute meaningfully. The idea is to seed the values, because you're going to get feedback from everyone else and complete it later.

You want to set the right tone, as well.

- Everyone's opinion matters. If half the people aren't contributing, you didn't encourage them enough.
- No one is right or wrong. All opinions are good, for now. Get into brainstorming mode where your goal is to create and suggest, not to edit or criticize. You can do the judging and evaluating later.

It's great if you have a whiteboard- or if you have to do it through an online meeting platform, have someone sharing their screen while taking notes.

Here's what you need to do:

1. **Personal Values Inventory**: Ask each participant to state their top three personal values, laying the foundation for what follows.
2. **Customer Insight:** Share the results of the customer values survey to introduce external perspectives.

3. **Corporate Values Discussion:** Prompt everyone to suggest values they believe are pivotal to the company's success.

4. **Equitable Participation:** Ensure each person speaks up, moderating the conversation to prevent any one individual from dominating.

5. **Live Compilation:** Record all proposed values on the whiteboard or shared screen, including the customer-derived values.

6. **Final Call for Input:** Once the brainstorming seems to wind down, ask if any values have been missed. Continue this process until no new values are suggested.

7. **Voting Process:** Each participant writes down their top three corporate values, which are then tallied to create a prioritized list. Give all that to one person to tabulate how many votes each value got. Update the whiteboard or notes document to show the number of votes for each.

Now you have a prioritized list of values from leadership.

Questions for Reflection:

- How will the leadership team maintain alignment with these values moving forward?
- What mechanisms can be implemented to ensure these values are communicated and adopted throughout the organization?

By following this process, you'll emerge with a list of prioritized values that reflect both internal and external perspectives, setting a strong foundation for aligned leadership and a cohesive corporate culture.

The All-Hands Meeting For Feedback and Improvement

The all-hands meeting is a pivotal moment in the process of updating your corporate values. It's an opportunity to bring every stakeholder into the conversation, from entry-level employees to upper management, to create a truly democratic and inclusive values list.

Not only are you going to get different perspectives, but you're also creating buy-in. Why? There's a chance that if the corporate values are dictated top-down, employees will feel disenfranchised and unrepresented. In that case, they're going to reject the values. Even if they don't say anything about it, their behaviors may not support the values later on.

However, if you give them a chance to contribute, you increase buy-in and the chances that these values will actually improve company performance, and employee and customer satisfaction.

So, to lead this meeting, you need to give some context. For example:

- "Thanks for coming. I'm glad you're all here."
- "We're looking forward to getting your input and helping us make these values accurate and powerful. We want them to reflect what's important to all of us, including customers."
- "These are going to be the values that we want to guide us on a daily basis. They'll help us make the best decisions for everyone."
- "We've already surveyed the customers, and a leadership group has started the process, but now, just as importantly, it's your turn to add things, question things, and do your own vote on what's most important."

Use this process for your meeting:

1. **Personal Values:** Invite volunteers to share their personal values, emphasizing the meeting's democratic nature. This is particularly important for

larger companies where it's impractical to hear from everyone.

2. **Customer Voices:** Share the results of the customer value survey to ensure that external perspectives are included in the discussion.

3. **Leadership's Draft List:** Present the list of values already identified by the leadership team, deliberately omitting how many votes each received to avoid biasing the discussion.

4. **Employee Input:** Open the floor for additional value suggestions. Continue this process until no new values are brought up.

5. **Employee Voting:** Each employee chooses their top three values. This can be done via a quick show of hands, electronic polling, or paper ballots, depending on the size and format of your meeting.

6. **Live Count, If Possible:** If it's manageable, count and announce the votes right there to enhance transparency. If not, assure everyone that the results will be communicated as soon as they are tabulated. A tip for you- it's almost impossible to count the raised hands; instead you can use a 1-3 scale. Imagine that a few hands is 1, almost all the hands is a 3, and a 2 is somewhere in between. Then you can quickly score each value with a 1, 2, or 3.

If you can't do so, conclude the meeting for now with these points:

- "Thank you everybody, we value your input."
- "Next, we're going to tabulate those votes. We'll send out an email with the results when we have them, and then we'll put it all together into a final list of prioritized values."

The Importance of Transparent Voting

Displaying the vote counts for each value can serve a dual purpose: It validates the democratic nature of the process and educates employees on the collective priorities. This can help individuals reconcile their personal values with those of the larger group, subtly increasing buy-in.

By adopting this comprehensive approach to the all-hands meeting, you not only encourage democratic participation but also enhance the likelihood that your updated corporate values will be embraced, respected, and effectively integrated into daily operations.

Integrating All The Input

After collecting inputs from multiple stakeholders—including leaders, employees, and customers—it's time to synthesize all that data into a cohesive list of values that reflects the whole organization. This critical step involves another leadership meeting and nuanced data analysis.

This is where you have another leadership meeting to put it all together. It doesn't have to be as big as your first leadership meeting, but if it's not, transparency matters even more. You'll want to share the details of the results with everyone later.

This is also an opportunity to see how customer values and how the original leadership group's prioritization of values varies from employees. We're going to combine them all, but you can also get some insight on potential management issues if you see any major differences between what leadership values vs the rest of the employees.

Pre-Meeting Preparations

- **Convert Votes to Percentages:** Given the discrepancy in the number of leaders and employees, switch to a percentage-based scoring system. For example, if a value received 30 out of 60 votes among leaders, it will have a score of 50. Leave off the percentage sign for simplification.

- **Equal Weighting:** Perform the same conversion for employee votes. This creates an 'apples-to-apples' comparison between leadership and employee values.
- **Create Scored Lists:** Prepare two scored, prioritized lists—one based on employee input and the other based on leadership input.
- **Combined Score:** Add the scores together for a combined list that takes into account everyone's perspectives.
- **Efficiency:** Complete these steps before the meeting to make the most of everyone's time.

Agenda for the Leadership Meeting

1. **Revisit Customer Values:** Make sure you haven't lost sight of the people who fuel your economic engine.
2. **Present Employee Values:** Share the scored and prioritized list of values based on employee input.
3. **Compare with Leadership Values:** Place this list alongside the leadership team's prioritized values.
4. **The Unified List:** Introduce the combined list that incorporates both sets of data.
5. **Critical Analysis and Discussion:** This is the time to scrutinize the list. Does anything seem amiss? Are there any glaring differences between what leadership and employees prioritize? Most importantly, do these values resonate with customer expectations?

Post-Meeting Actions

1. **Finalize the List:** Once there's a consensus, the final list can be ratified.
2. **Simplify for Consumption:** While the complete list is essential for internal reference, consider distilling it down to the top 5-7 values for easier consumption.

3. **Communication:** Share the final lists, both complete and simplified, with the entire organization. This could be done through company-wide emails, intranet postings, or even a follow-up all-hands meeting.
4. **Transparency:** Also, share how these values were arrived at, highlighting the democratic process to bolster buy-in.

Monitoring and Feedback

Pay attention to how these newly defined values are received and integrated into day-to-day work. Regularly revisit these values to ensure they remain aligned with organizational goals and stakeholder expectations.

By using this systematic approach, you ensure that the corporate values aren't just a top-down mandate but a reflection of the collective intelligence and aspirations of the entire organization.

22. Follow-Thru: Implement and Enforce Values for Long-Term Success

As I said earlier, if your values are simply lost deep in your website, they won't do you any good. People can't follow what they're not aware of. Even if they're on the wall at the entrance to your building and people know what they are, that still doesn't mean they'll have an effect on your everyday actions and decisions.

The good news is that if you followed the Values Update process, it should be easy for you to implement a some of the new values- they came from you, in part. For some people, these values will be natural, and for others, perhaps those who were in the minority, they won't. So it will require some dedication and work.

Plus, it may be new for you to make decisions based on the priority of the values.

Here's an example: we worked with a marketing company whose top three values turned out to be:

1. Trust
2. Impact
3. Adaptability

So when they considered ways to make impact, they had to make sure none of them eroded trust. That can be as straightforward as not making ethical compromises to get what leaders, employees, or customers want. That means, for example, considering how customers respond to telemarketing and various degrees of spam, even when they are legal and produce impact. If those approaches decrease trust in the brand, they're not worth doing, given the corporation has placed trust at the top.

When this company thought about how to adapt to changes in the market, they had to adapt in a way that maintained or increased impact, and didn't erode trust. That could include things like responding to how Millennial or Gen Z buyers are different from previous generations, but without offending them, and without hurting their trustworthiness with Gen X or Boomers.

You may value increasing revenues and profits and want to improve those by subscribing every new customer to 10 different email lists. Even if you put your intention to do this into the fine print of your terms of service (which no one reads), if it annoys your customers, this subtle version of spam could decrease trust and overall impact.

Management can have issues with impact vs trust, as well, for example, with micromanagement. There are many ways to think about, approach, and even monitor with technology that can be perceived as micromanagement, and typically employees can respond with anger. Their complaint is that management doesn't trust them. And if that affects productivity, culture, and turnover, then micromanagement has not only hurt trust, but also hasn't had a positive impact.

An important distinction is which your organization values more: profit or people. Yes, you have to choose one over the other- that's the nature of prioritizing- it forces us to make value-decisions ahead of time so that individual decisions are quicker, easier, and more widely supported by the culture. If each value isn't on its own priority line, you're going to have unresolvable arguments, or at least arguments whose resolution isn't satisfying to a significant number of people. Better to be bold with your priorities in your Value Update process, and if anyone finds them disturbing, let that person move to another organization that suits them better.

If both work-life balance and profits are two of your top values, there may be times where layoffs and increasing workloads increase profits but hurt work-life balance. In that case, if work-life balance is a major retention factor, turnover and hiring costs can increase, eating into your profits anyway.

If profits are valued higher than work-life balance and retention, this becomes a matter of calculation- what do your accounting metrics say about those two scenario? But when valuing people is more important to you than profits, other measures like employee happiness surveying and scoring will be paramount.

I'm not here to make any judgments or push my values onto you and your organization. Just make sure you make decisions according to your prioritized values, and be consistent.

And it's ok over time, as you see how decisions play out, to go back and revise the values and priorities. Let customer, employee, and leadership feedback further refine them.

Embedding Corporate Values in Daily Operations

Understanding corporate values is one thing; making them matter in everyday operations is another. Values can be easy to forget amidst the hustle and bustle of work. To make sure they're consistently lived, breathed, and used for decision-making, you'll need a proactive approach. Here's a guide to making your corporate values a functional part of your organization's daily life.

1. The Meeting Advocate for Values

- **Role:** Appoint a dedicated person in every meeting whose job it is to align the discussion and decisions with the company's prioritized values.
- **How It Works:** This person observes the meeting's flow and, when they notice a value being discussed or enacted, they point it out. They also bring relevant values into focus during hard decisions.
- **Impact:** This constant reminder serves to infuse values into all facets of the business, making them more than just words on a page.

2. Manager-Employee Value Check-Ins

During one-on-ones or performance reviews, managers should raise the topic of corporate values. Ask questions like:

"How have you seen the corporate values reflected in your work recently?"

"Have you had to make any challenging decisions where our corporate values were relevant?"

The goal isn't to catch employees making incorrect choices, but to facilitate a dialog that models how to apply corporate values in decision-making.

Tips for Individual and Collective Action

- **Daily Reminders:** Whether it's a poster on the wall, a note in the daily newsletter, or an app notification, find ways to remind employees of the corporate values regularly.
- **Role Modeling:** Leaders and managers should embody these values, demonstrating what it looks like when decisions are made according to the corporate value list.
- **Reward and Recognition:** Acknowledge and celebrate when team members exemplify a corporate value exceptionally well, thus reinforcing its importance.

Consistency is Key

To maintain the impact and relevance of your corporate values:

- **Ongoing Reinforcement:** The values need to be reinforced continually through actions, communications, and in the decision-making process.
- **Periodic Review:** Just as the business evolves, so should your values. Make it a practice to review them regularly to ensure they are still aligned with your corporate strategy and culture.

By implementing these guidelines, you're not just paying lip service to your values; you're embedding them in the company's DNA. This not only upholds the integrity of the company but also contributes to a more cohesive, productive, and joyful workplace.

The Research

Here are five recommendations for how to make corporate values matter day-to-day at work:

- Communicate your values clearly and consistently to your employees1236. Make sure that your employees understand what your company values are and how they should be reflected in their day-to-day work. Use various communication channels such as company meetings, newsletters, and training sessions to reinforce your values.

- Lead by example136. Your leadership team should embody your company values and set the tone for the rest of the organization. Make sure that your leaders are modeling the behavior that you want to see in your employees.

- Recognize and reward employees who demonstrate your company values136. Acknowledge and celebrate employees who embody your values in their work. This will reinforce the importance of your values and motivate other employees to follow suit.

- Incorporate your values into your performance management process136. Make sure that your employees' performance goals and evaluations are aligned with your company values. This will help ensure that your values are being reflected in your employees' day-to-day work.

- Continuously evaluate and refine your values2356. Your company values should be dynamic and evolve over time. Regularly assess whether your values are still relevant and meaningful to your organization. Solicit feedback from your employees and stakeholders to ensure that your values are aligned with your business objectives.

References:

1. Haiilo. (2023). Company Values: Definition, Importance and Examples.
2. Lesley University. (2019). The Power of Company Core Values.
3. Forbes. (2021). Why Core Values Matter (And How To Get Your Team Excited About Them).
4. Gallup. (2022). Are Your Company Values More Than Just Words?
5. Plai.team. What are company values and why they are important.

Part IV: Actionable Strategies for Retention and Satisfaction

The multi-generational workplace is a melting pot of values, experiences, and communication styles—or shall we say, a bubbling cauldron waiting to either concoct the perfect potion or explode? Isn't it time to transform that cauldron into a symphony of orchestrated teamwork?

There are a lot of issues. Feel free to jump around the remainder of this book and focus on what you need most.

Communication and Teamwork

23. Conflict: How Specific Generations Fight

Why do office hallways sometimes echo with discordant notes? What if we could transform them into collaborative symphonies?

Inter-generational conflicts in the workplace can stem from differences in values, communication styles, technological proficiency, expectations, and work habits. While generalizing specific traits to entire generations can be limiting and potentially inaccurate, certain observable trends and studies have pointed out patterns in inter-generational conflicts.

Here's a breakdown:

Silent Generation

Potential Conflicts: May be perceived as resistant to change or new technologies, may prefer a top-down approach to management. Imagine Beethoven trying to compose electronic dance music. That's how they may feel about new technologies.

Common Conflicts with: Baby Boomers (over leadership styles) and Millennials or Gen Z (over technology usage). Silent Gen'ers sometimes strike the wrong chord with Baby Boomers over leadership styles, and with Millennials and Gen Z over digital fluency.

Baby Boomers

Potential Conflicts: Might place high value on loyalty and long hours, may prefer face-to-face communication, and can be perceived as resistant to new technologies. Picture a Jazz musician who has mastered the classics, yet is criticized for not adopting new-age tunes.

Common Conflicts with: Gen X (regarding work-life balance) and Millennials (around topics of commitment and loyalty). They can clash with Gen X over improvising work-life balance, and with Millennials over long-term membership in the "band."

Generation X

Potential Conflicts: Highly value work-life balance, might be skeptical of authority figures, may prefer to work independently. Imagine a guitarist who values both the spotlight and the green room, with others questioning this dual love.

Common Conflicts with: Baby Boomers (around commitment and the importance of face time at the office) and Millennials (concerning feedback and communication styles). They may find themselves in a rock-and-hard-place situation with Boomers over face-time in the studio, and Millennials over creative input.

Millennials/Gen Y

Potential Conflicts: May expect regular feedback, can be perceived as wanting to "climb the ladder" quickly, highly value flexibility, are digital natives and thus highly reliant on technology. Think of them as DJs, always sampling from other genres but eager for real-time feedback to perfect their tracks.

Common Conflicts with: Baby Boomers and Gen X (over communication styles, the need for flexibility, and differing views on loyalty and job-hopping). They can get into a lyrical feud with Boomers and Gen X over the preferred channels of feedback, whether face-to-face or via social media.

Generation Z

Potential Conflicts: Highly technologically proficient, have short attention spans due to the digital age, desire authenticity and social responsibility. Picture them as mixers and producers who craft soundscapes in digital studios.

Common Conflicts with: Older generations over their reliance on technology for almost everything and their changing views on job roles and corporate responsibility. Gen Z's modern beats sometimes challenge the more traditional artists who stick to acoustic instruments, creating a divide over technological approaches.

General Areas of Conflict

- **Technology:** Older generations may struggle with or resist new technology, while younger generations may become impatient with the perceived technological shortcomings of their older colleagues. Vintage synthesizers versus AI-driven mixing tables; a clash of tools but not of craftsmanship.

- **Communication:** Preferences vary widely, from face-to-face meetings preferred by older generations to the instantaneous digital communication favored by younger ones. Is it vinyl records or Spotify playlists? A disagreement over mediums but not messages.

- **Feedback:** Older generations might be accustomed to less frequent, formal feedback, while Millennials and Gen Z may desire constant, informal feedback. Do we need an annual review like the Grammys, or a continuous stream of SoundCloud comments?

- **Work Ethic and Loyalty:** Older generations might view younger workers as lacking commitment, while younger generations might view longer tenures as a lack of ambition or adaptability. Is loyalty sticking to one label or exploring collaborations across the industry?
- **Work-Life Balance:** Prioritization of work-life balance can vary, with younger generations often placing a higher emphasis on this. The eternal debate between life on the road and time in the studio.
- **Values and Motivations:** Younger generations might prioritize companies with social responsibility, while older generations might prioritize job security and benefits. Is the ultimate goal a lifetime achievement award or a hit that drives social change?

Let's not forget, this is an orchestra where every musician has a unique tone. Could training and awareness be the conductor that unifies these varied instruments? Absolutely, and it should be. For in this diversity lies not a cacophony but a symphony of possibilities.

Not everyone within a generation will fit these patterns, and individual differences often outweigh generational ones. Effective training and awareness can help address and bridge these generational gaps, emphasizing the strengths each group brings to the table and fostering a more inclusive and harmonious workplace.

By adopting this modern framework, you're better able to understand the challenges and turn them into opportunities, all while resonating with the collective sentiments of each generation. Isn't that the first step towards creating an inclusive, harmonious workplace?

24. Teamwork: Solve Common Issues for a Unified Workforce

Why do generational divides seem like chasms, not cracks? Imagine being a bridge builder, not just an observer—laying down the planks of understanding between two cliffs that have never been connected.

First, know what each generation values. But also, consider how they were raised and taught to communicate. Here are some tips for each generation:

Silent Generation (Born before 1945):

Respect Above All: Picture an old library—its silence, its dignity. That's what respect and formalities feel like to a Traditionalist. Call them by their titles; let them know their experience is a book everyone wants to read. They value hard work, dedication, and respect for authority. Address them by titles, and show respect for their experience.

Old-School Connection: Imagine sending a handwritten thank-you letter. For them, this is not archaic; it's sincere and thoughtful. They might prefer more traditional forms of communication, so personal meetings or written letters could be effective.

Share stories: Think of them as storytellers around a bonfire. Their stories are their lived experiences, waiting to be shared.

Baby Boomers (1946-1964):

The Power of Presence: Picture a business meeting from a 1990s movie—suits, handshakes, and eye contact. Baby Boomers thrive on that in-person chemistry.

Tech-Savvy, Not Tech-Averse: Think they can't handle a Zoom call? Think again. They may even show you a thing or two about PowerPoint animations.

A Repository of Experience: Imagine them as the village elders; their life lessons are the community's treasure.

Gen X (1965-1980):

Straight to the Point: Imagine a bullet list in human form. They want the facts, not the fluff.

The Best of Both Worlds: Like a good mixtape, they're a balance of analogue and digital.

Flexibility as a Mantra: Picture a gymnast gracefully executing a routine—that's how they approach work-life balance.

Millennials (1981-1996):

The Digital Natives: Imagine growing up in a world where a touchscreen is as common as a notepad. Texting and emailing are their second language.

The Team Spirit: Think of a team huddle in a sport— they live for the communal "1, 2, 3, let's go!"

Feedback Hungry: Envision them as artists, their work not complete until critiqued and refined.

The Greater Good: Picture a protest or a movement; they're in the center, advocating for what they believe brings purpose.

Gen Z (1997-2012):

Short and Snappy: Imagine a Twitter feed or TikTok stream—brief, but impactful.

Diverse in Platform, Unified in Interest: Picture them navigating through apps like sailors through archipelagos—each island different, yet familiar.

Inclusion and Realness: Think of them as the curators of a human museum; they celebrate all forms of authentic expression.

Now, Not Later: Imagine a ticking clock; that's how they view communication.

Universal Commandments Across All Ages

- **Empathy is King:** What would it be like to step into their shoes? Make the effort to understand, to really get it.

- **The Preferred Frequency:** Just as you have your favorite radio station, they have their preferred ways of communicating. Have you asked them theirs?
- **Keep Riding the Wave:** Ever tried catching up with a runaway train? That's what trying to catch up with digital trends feels like. Stay ahead, and you'll never have to catch up.

This roadmap is not a one-size-fits-all but a palette of strategies. It's up to you to paint the masterpiece that is effective communication. So, can we pave this road, span these chasms, and build these bridges together? Yes, we can. And yes, we will.

25. Impact: Teach Universal Communication Skills for Optimal Effectiveness

Why do some conversations with colleagues feel like navigating a maze, while others flow like a well-timed symphony? What's the secret sauce that can lead any conversation to a crescendo of understanding and action?

Giving credit where credit is due, this is a synopsis of a tool that has served me well since I learned it 20+ years ago, created by Matthew McKay PhD, Martha Davis PhD, and Patrick Fanning, and fully elaborated on in *Messages: The Communication Skills Book*. I highly recommend it.

The tool is called "Whole Messages."

The Four Pillars of Whole Messages

In the architectural language of communication, think of Whole Messages as a resilient structure built on four cornerstones:

1. **Facts:** The blueprint or ground plan of the conversation. These are the irrefutable, evidence-based realities that set the stage for any discussion.
2. **Thoughts:** The intricate design details, your perspectives and opinions that make the conversation unique.
3. **Feelings:** The ambiance and emotional environment of the conversation. Are we standing in a serene Zen garden or navigating a tumultuous storm?
4. **Needs:** The purpose or end-goal, the final touches that make the structure both functional and aesthetically pleasing.

Can a house stand on a single pillar? Imagine:

- **Facts Alone:** If you don't give people context (facts) for your thoughts and feelings, they may just think you're crazy. A barren plot of land without a building.

Yes, it's a real piece of land, but what are you going to do with it?

- **Thoughts without Context:** An abstract art installation in the middle of nowhere. It may be beautiful or striking, but it's not grounded in any discernible reality.
- **Feelings without Direction:** Picture a labyrinthine garden. It may be emotionally stirring, but if you're lost, what's the point?
- **Needs without Clarity:** A half-finished building. Without knowing what's needed to complete it, how can anyone assist?

Doesn't a conversation reach its pinnacle of effectiveness when facts are recognized, thoughts are understood, feelings are validated, and needs are mutually addressed? Absolutely.

And just like in a musical ensemble, when every member knows their part—when the trumpets and violins, the drums and the flutes all play in harmony—that's when we create something transcendent.

Could this simple but profound tool be the Rosetta Stone for translating the unique languages of Silent Gen'ers, Baby Boomers, Gen X, Millennials, and Gen Z into a single, cohesive narrative? This could be the key to setting high and ambitious goals for communication across generations and achieving them with confidence.

So, are we ready to conduct this symphony?

By imparting this framework to all employees, regardless of their generational cohort, we can all orchestrate meaningful dialogues that not only hit the right notes but also create a melody that resounds across the entire organization.

26. Exercises: Use Smart Team-Building to Boost Morale

Striving for a new pinnacle of organizational achievement? Aim high. Transform your workplace from a group of siloed individuals into a cohesive, happy team. And yes, you can accomplish this in a way that resonates with everyone, from the baby boomers to Gen Z.

Imagine your team as a well-oiled machine—each gear uniquely contoured, yet meshing perfectly with its neighbors. The hum of contentment and morale is what keeps the machine from grinding to a halt. Activities like high fives and fist bumps can lubricate those gears, thanks to oxytocin and mirror neurons.

I knew a manager who, burdened by team turnover, decided to focus solely on performance metrics. The situation worsened. Then, a switch to morale-boosting activities was flipped. Performance soared. This is more than a story; it's a blueprint for emotional investment in your team.

Why do we often ignore the relationship between team morale and productivity? Are we stuck in outdated paradigms that value individual output over collective harmony? These are not just questions but challenges to our ingrained ways of thinking.

Forget the old notions that say hard skills trump soft skills or that numbers speak louder than words. The reality? It's not either-or; it's both. A paradigm shift towards the balance of hard skills and emotional intelligence can make all the difference.

- Boost oxytocin and engage mirror neurons through high fives and fist bumps.
- Foster teamwork through board games like Pictionary.
- Enliven the atmosphere with funny role-playing exercises.

The ethical cornerstone? Team morale isn't just about profits or performance; it's about creating a culture of mutual respect and happiness. High morale often leads to high ethical standards.

We've all been there—trapped in soul-crushing meetings, yearning for some spark of excitement or, at the very least, mutual understanding. It doesn't have to be that way. Smart team-building activities can revitalize your workplace, making it a setting where people are not just eager to work but eager to work together.

Remember, this isn't just theory. Phrases like "let's give it our all" or "we're in this together" can serve as anchors that make these ideas tangible, offering a constant reminder to keep the morale high.

Ever wondered what would happen if your team started each day with a team-building exercise? Or if there was a "no-phone lunch hour" for a week? Engage in these hypothetical scenarios, and you might just find the morale and productivity soaring.

The time to foster team morale is now. Take action. Revitalize your team and by extension, your entire organization. Embrace the exercises listed, watch the morale soar, and prepare to reap the numerous benefits that come with a happy, cohesive team.

But a word of caution:

You've been there—the awkward team-building exercises that feel forced and uninspiring. Whether it's trust falls that instill fear more than trust or icebreakers that leave everyone cringing, unimaginative exercises can backfire dramatically. Far from boosting morale, they can create an environment of dread and apprehension. The irony is that these activities, designed to bring people closer, often drive a wedge between team members and deepen generational divides.

Why does this happen? Generic exercises often miss the mark because they lack relatability. The activities that might resonate with a Gen X'er might not necessarily appeal to a Millennial or a Gen Z employee. Moreover, these one-size-fits-all exercises tend to ignore the diverse skill sets and interests that people bring to the table. The result is a formulaic approach that lacks authenticity and creativity, contributing to a sense of detachment and worsening team morale.

So how do we navigate this tricky terrain and create team-building activities that everyone can buy into? First, consider inclusivity. Rather than implementing a standard set of exercises, why not take the time to understand the different personalities, preferences, and generational inclinations in your team? Use surveys or direct discussions to gauge what kinds of activities your team would actually find engaging.

Secondly, create a variety of options. Offer both introspective exercises for the more analytical minds and active, playful activities for those who prefer physical engagement. The aim is to create a menu of team-building exercises that cater to different needs yet share the same objective—strengthening team bonds and boosting morale.

Finally, be ready to pivot. An openness to feedback and the agility to make adjustments can go a long way in ensuring the long-term success of your team-building initiatives. In a dynamic workplace where team compositions and project requirements are constantly changing, your approach to boosting morale should be equally fluid.

By avoiding cliché and uninspiring activities, focusing on inclusivity, and remaining flexible, you're not just boosting morale for the sake of it. You're sending a message that each team member's comfort and engagement are priorities, worth taking the time to get right. This inclusive and thoughtful approach doesn't just lift spirits; it fosters a culture where everyone feels valued, and that's the ultimate win for any team.

Action Steps

1. Initiate "High Five Fridays" to encourage physical gestures of camaraderie- as long as they're workplace appropriate!
2. Arrange bi-weekly team games, starting with Pictionary.
3. Implement a funny role-playing session once a month.
4. Hand out quarterly awards recognizing each team member's unique contribution.
5. Schedule regular coffee breaks and phone-free lunches to facilitate genuine conversation.

So, are we ready to reevaluate and re-energize our approach to team-building? Are we committed to breaking away from clichés and mind-numbing activities that serve no real purpose other than to fill time? These questions aren't just provocations—they're invitations to take immediate action.

Today is the day to begin this transformation. Put aside the old playbook and start crafting team-building exercises that truly resonate with your team's diverse makeup and needs. Conduct that survey, create that "menu" of varied exercises, and open the channels for ongoing feedback. Don't just settle for temporary boosts in morale; aim for lasting change that transforms your organizational culture. In doing so, you won't just be elevating team spirit; you'll be setting the stage for unparalleled success and productivity. Act now, and watch your team—and your organization—thrive.

The Research

Scientific findings and recommendations for effective team-building exercises:

- Team building exercises can have measurable, positive effects on team performance[26].
- Exercises designed to build interpersonal relationships and enhance problem-solving abilities are most effective[3].

- Effective team building requires buy-in from team members[3].
- Team building exercises should allow teams to tackle an achievable challenge together[3].
- Team building exercises that focus on the sharing of, and intervening into personal attitudes and relationships between team members may be considered too invasive and not effective[3].
- Multidisciplinary teams produce better quality innovations than more uniform teams, but team leaders need to ensure that each member feels included[2].
- Teamwork interventions that involve workshop-style exercises involving all team members, such as working through case studies, watching and critiquing video vignettes, and practicing teamwork skills, are effective at enhancing teamwork and team performance[6].

References

1. Small Group Research. (2009). Does Team Building Work?
2. Full Focus. (2018). The Science of Teambuilding.
3. ScienceDaily. (2021). Benefits of team building exercises jeopardized if not truly voluntary.
4. Salas, E., Diaz-Granados, D., Klein, C., Burke, C. S., Stagl, K. C., Goodwin, G. F., & Halpin, S. M. (2008). The Effectiveness of Teamwork Training on Teamwork Behaviors and Team Performance: A Systematic Review and Meta-Analysis of Controlled Interventions. National Center for Biotechnology Information.

27. Compromise: Encourage Youthful Flexibility for a Harmonious Environment

Getting younger people – or anyone, for that matter – to compromise at work involves a combination of understanding, clear communication, and skillful negotiation.

Consider younger employees as pioneers exploring a new frontier. They arrive equipped with fresh perspectives and tools that you might not be familiar with. But, as any seasoned explorer knows, a successful expedition requires teamwork.

Here are several strategies to encourage compromise. Let's view these strategies as navigational stars in the sky, guiding us through the journey of compromise.

Before asking for compromise, ensure that you've built a foundation of trust. When individuals trust you, they are more likely to see the value in your perspective and be willing to find middle ground. Consider this the North Star. A solid relationship based on trust is the celestial body that guides all other navigation.

Understand where they're coming from. Younger individuals may have different priorities or viewpoints shaped by their unique experiences or the times they've grown up in. Listen without interrupting, ask questions, and try to understand their perspective fully. Imagine this as your compass. You can't move in the right direction without knowing where the other person is coming from.

Sometimes younger employees may not have the historical context of why certain decisions were made in the past. Offering this context can help them understand the broader picture. Think of this as your map, outlining the lay of the land based on past expeditions. New explorers may not have this historical perspective; share it with them.

If compromise is a ship, let them be your co-captain. When people feel ownership, they are more committed to steering the ship safely to its destination. When people feel they have a stake in the decision or that their opinions are valued, they are more likely to compromise. Make them part of the solution.

Emphasize the common goals and how the compromise benefits everyone, not just one side. This is the mutual destination that everyone on the expedition agrees to reach.

Sometimes the seas are too rough for sailing. Wait for the right moment to embark on the journey of compromise. If someone is stressed, tired, or otherwise not in the best state of mind, it's probably not the best time to seek compromise. Find a time when both parties can be calm and focused.

Offer training in conflict resolution, negotiation, and communication. This can be particularly helpful in organizations where compromise and collaboration are essential. Picture this as your survival kit, containing tools like conflict resolution and negotiation skills that are essential for the journey ahead.

Sometimes, a lack of compromise stems from not understanding what's expected. Make sure roles, responsibilities, and expectations are clear. This is your travel itinerary. Ensure everyone knows the route and the stops along the way.

If you were to send scouts ahead to gather information, this would be it. Keep the channels of communication open. Allow younger employees to voice their concerns and provide feedback. This will not only help you understand their perspective better, but they'll also appreciate that they're being heard.

Demonstrate compromise in your actions. When employees, regardless of their age, see leaders compromising and being flexible, they are more likely to adopt similar behaviors. When the captain navigates skillfully, the crew learns. Be that exemplary captain.

When a compromise leads to a successful outcome, celebrate it. This is the feast you have when you find the missing piece of the map or reach an important milestone. This reinforces the idea that collaboration and compromise can lead to positive results.

Sometimes, you need an experienced guide to help traverse treacherous terrain. Don't hesitate to seek one when needed. If a compromise is challenging to reach, consider involving a neutral third party to facilitate the discussion.

Every individual is different. No two explorers are alike. Your compass must be attuned to the unique aspirations, motivations, and concerns of each individual. Consider their personal motivations, aspirations, and concerns, and adapt your approach accordingly.

Is compromise just about meeting halfway? Or could it be the bridge that unites the new frontier with the tried-and-true landscapes of old, benefiting everyone involved?

Can we not only recognize the individual melodies each generation plays but also harmonize them into a symphony of collective achievement?

In the grand scheme of things, learning how to compromise effectively—especially with younger generations—will not only solve immediate problems but also enrich the workplace culture. It's a win-win scenario, or shall we say, the treasure at the end of our mutual expedition.

The Research

7 recommendations on how coworkers can compromise:

- Share all appropriate and relevant information and avoid being vague[1].
- Ask open-ended questions to maintain a safe environment[1].
- Identify and manage conflicts of interest to achieve research goals[2,3,4].
- Place limits on involvement of faculty members and other institutional officials in companies[3].
- Exercise caution when technology-transfer official's remuneration is tied to stock values[3].
- Manage and review conflicts of interest using independent sources and external reviewers[3].
- Enhance the effectiveness of work groups and teams by focusing on key areas in which theory and research findings are well developed[6].

References

1. Stone, D., Patton, B., & Heen, S. (2010). Difficult conversations: How to discuss what matters most. Penguin.
2. Resnik, D. B. (2015). Conflicts of interest in research: looking out for number one means keeping the primary interest front and center. Journal of Clinical Investigation, 125(5), 1411-1413.
3. Bradley, S. G. (2000). Managing Conflicting Interests. In F. L. Magrina (Ed.), Scientific Integrity: An Introductory Text with Cases (pp. 131-157). American Society for Microbiology.
4. University of Southern California. (2013). Conflict of Interest in Research.
5. Li, J., & Su, Y. (2007). The relationship between "face" and reference group norms. Journal of Social Psychology, 147(2), 165-178.
6. Kozlowski, S. W. J., & Ilgen, D. R. (2006). Enhancing the effectiveness of work groups and teams. Psychological Science in the Public Interest, 7(3), 77-124.

Employee Satisfaction and Well-Being

28. Joy: Discover the Secrets to Workplace Happiness

Imagine a championship-winning sports team. Each player, from rookies to seasoned veterans, has individual needs, strengths, and preferences. Yet, when they're on the field, they're all guided by a single aim: to win. Let's delve into the playbook that coaches and organizations can use to make sure everyone on their "team" is satisfied, engaged, and giving their best.

People's happiness at work can be influenced by a variety of factors, both intrinsic and extrinsic. Here are some of the most common factors that contribute to workplace satisfaction.

We need purpose and meaning. Feeling that one's work has purpose and contributes to a greater good can provide a strong sense of fulfillment. Consider this the championship trophy everyone is striving for, the ultimate goal that makes all the hard work and sacrifice meaningful.

Autonomy is important. This is like a player who specializes in free-kicks or three-pointers. They need room to use their special skills but also need to be part of the overall game strategy. Being able to have some control over one's tasks, schedule, and methods can lead to increased job satisfaction.

Using and developing one's skills and talents can make work more enjoyable. Think of this as a player being positioned where their skills shine the most—say, a great passer in the midfield or an excellent rebounder under the basketball hoop.

Knowing exactly what's expected in one's job role can reduce stress and ambiguity. Just as in sports, where each player knows their position and role—whether it's a quarterback, defender, or striker—clear guidelines lead to effective teamwork.

Feedback and recognition help. This is your post-game analysis and MVP awards; recognition for excellent performance boosts morale and encourages continuous improvement. Regular, constructive feedback and recognition for achievements can boost morale.

Positive relationships with colleagues, managers, and subordinates contribute significantly to job satisfaction. A supportive team environment is particularly important. Team chemistry is key. Whether it's celebrating a touchdown or supporting a teammate after a mistake, strong bonds enhance group dynamics.

Being able to balance work demands with personal life is critical for overall well-being. Players need time for rest and recovery, too. Overworking leads to burnout, affecting not just individual performance but the entire team's.

Receiving a salary and benefits that reflect one's work and responsibilities is a significant factor. Just as star athletes negotiate contracts that reflect their market value, employees need to feel that their contribution is fairly rewarded.

Opportunities for personal and professional development, including training and career advancement, can be motivating. Think of this as offseason training camps and skill development courses, helping players improve and prepare for the next season.

Feeling secure in one's position and having trust in the company's stability can reduce anxiety. Much like a multi-year contract, knowing that they're part of the team's long-term plans can boost a player's confidence and focus.

A good coach knows how to manage diverse talents, keep morale high, and help the team adapt to new challenges. Competent, understanding, and communicative management can make a huge difference in an employee's work experience.

A safe, comfortable, and aesthetically pleasing workspace can enhance mood and productivity. Think of this as the quality of the training facilities, the locker room, or even the home stadium. A good environment boosts performance.

Working for an organization whose values and mission align with one's own can be fulfilling. This is like playing for a team that stands for something you believe in, whether it's community outreach or a particular playing philosophy.

Having a mix of tasks and responsibilities can prevent monotony and burnout. A well-rounded team plays both offense and defense, tackles both easy and challenging opponents, and brings diversity to the playing field.

challenges that are tough but achievable can be motivating and lead to a sense of accomplishment. These are the landmark games or key moments in the season that test the team's mettle but also bring the most satisfaction when successfully navigated.

Different individuals might prioritize these factors differently based on their personal values, career stage, and life circumstances. It's important for employers to recognize and address these factors to promote employee well-being and productivity.

Is your employee an eager rookie or a seasoned veteran? What makes them excited to get into the game? Understanding each player's motivations and adapting your coaching style to them can significantly boost team morale and performance.

Workplace happiness isn't just about executing individual plays well; it's about creating a cohesive, motivated team that is prepared to tackle any challenge and pursue every opportunity. The result is not just individual satisfaction but collective success.

The Research

Here are seven findings on happiness at work supported by scholarly academic research:

- Motivating job characteristics are positively related to happiness at work[2].
- Growth mindsets about the self and job can increase happiness at work[3].
- Feeling appreciated by coworkers predicts happiness at work[3].

- Enjoyment of daily tasks significantly predicts happiness at work[3].
- Meaningful work is positively related to happiness at work[3].
- Psychological capital is positively related to workplace happiness and well-being[4].
- Happiness at work is a combination of pleasure, engagement, and meaning[1].

References

1. Oerlemans, W. G. M., & Bakker, A. B. (2018). Motivating job characteristics and happiness at work: A multilevel perspective.

2. Nguyen, T.-D. (2021). Making work a happy practice. In J. Marques (Ed.), The Routledge companion to happiness at work.

3. Charles-Leija, H., Castro, C. G., Toledo, M., & Ballesteros-Valdés, R. (2023). Meaningful Work, Happiness at Work, and Turnover Intentions. International Journal of Environmental Research and Public Health, 20(4), 1191.

4. Kun, A., & Gadanecz, P. (2022). Workplace happiness, well-being and their relationship with psychological capital: A study of Hungarian teachers.

29. Compensation: Reward Young Talent in Ways that Matter

Too many companies try everything else but ensuring their employees have up-to-date fair market competitive compensation, and suffer for it.

Imagine two mountains, one significantly taller than the other. The taller mountain represents the older generation, settled in their jobs, comfortable, and well-compensated. The shorter mountain, meanwhile, symbolizes the younger generation—just as eager, just as talented, but still in the foothills of their career. They strive to climb to similar heights but are grappling with steeper inclines and lesser resources.

The soil of discontent among young workers is fertile, nourished by several catalysts—financial pressure, wage inequality, career concerns, and rising expenses, to name a few. This isn't a mere list; these are the voices of a generation calling for change.

Work compensation being a big issue for young people can be attributed to several factors.

Young people often face significant financial pressures due to student loans, high cost of living, and the need to establish themselves. Adequate compensation is crucial for them to cover their expenses and work towards financial stability.

Young workers, especially those just entering the job market, may face wage inequality and a wage gap compared to older, more experienced colleagues. This can be frustrating and discouraging, especially if they perceive their compensation as not reflecting their skills and contributions.

The cost of education, housing, healthcare, and other essential services has been rising, and young people are acutely aware of this. If compensation doesn't keep pace with these rising expenses, it can lead to dissatisfaction and frustration.

Young workers are often concerned about their future career growth and financial stability. If they feel they are being underpaid early in their careers, they might worry that this could impact their earning potential in the long term.

Many young people are in temporary or contract positions that may not offer the same benefits and job security as full-time roles. This lack of stability can make the issue of compensation even more pressing, as they may not have the same safety net as more established workers.

Young workers might feel that their contributions and skills are undervalued, especially if they are in positions where they have to prove themselves. This can lead to frustration if their compensation doesn't align with the effort and value they believe they are bringing to the organization.

The modern work landscape is changing rapidly due to advancements in technology and shifts in work patterns. Young people may have different expectations about work-life balance, remote work options, and benefits, and they may be pushing for compensation packages that align with these changing priorities.

With increased access to information through the internet and social media, young people are more aware of compensation disparities and workplace practices. They may be more inclined to advocate for fair compensation, especially if they see their peers or colleagues in similar roles receiving better compensation elsewhere.

Young people often carry student loan debt, which can be a substantial financial burden. They may feel that their compensation should help them manage this debt effectively, especially if their education was a significant investment.

Young people might have a stronger sense of social justice and fairness, and they may be more willing to speak out against perceived injustices, including inadequate compensation.

Addressing these concerns involves creating transparent compensation structures, offering avenues for career growth, and valuing the contributions of young workers appropriately.

Do We Value Potential or Just Experience?

Many young professionals enter the job market armed with credentials and brimming with potential. Shouldn't their compensation reflect this promise and not just years on a resume?

Meet Sarah, a millennial, and Tom, a baby boomer. They both work in marketing for the same company. Sarah is highly skilled in digital marketing, a field Tom is not familiar with. Yet, Tom's compensation is significantly higher than Sarah's. While experience counts, the question is: Are we undermining the importance of specialized skills that younger employees often bring to the table?

The older generation usually has the advantage of job security and higher wages. Contrastingly, younger workers face insecure job positions and stagnant wages. To bridge this gap, both sides must be willing to move toward the center, valuing both experience and fresh skills.

Addressing this imbalance isn't just smart business—it's a moral obligation. It's about acknowledging the worth of every individual, regardless of their career stage.

We should listen not just to individual stories of wage discontent but to the collective sentiment of a generation yearning for a more equitable workplace.

Imagine a future where salary transparency is the norm, where career growth is not a nebulous concept but a clearly defined path. This is not an impossible dream but a realistic goal that we should strive for.

How do we achieve this future? By leveraging online tools like Salary.com and Indeed's Salaries, we empower both employers and employees with data, demystifying compensation rates, and thus taking a crucial step toward a more equitable workplace.

Let's picture a world where Sarah and Tom earn salaries that accurately reflect their skills and contributions. In this world, Sarah feels valued and empowered, thereby becoming more productive and engaged. Tom, recognizing the fairness, is content and appreciative of Sarah's skills. Everyone wins.

Addressing these concerns of young workers does not mean disadvantaging the older generation. It simply means creating a balanced, transparent environment where each person's value is recognized.

By considering the market rate, incorporating it into a transparent compensation structure, and providing avenues for career growth, we're not just paying people; we're investing in a future where everyone's worth is acknowledged and celebrated.

The Research

Here are six findings about employee compensation:

- Financial compensation can have a significant impact on employee motivation[2].
- Pay-for-performance systems can increase productivity and task completion rates[4].
- Total compensation management can be an effective strategy for attracting and retaining employees[3].
- Base pay, pay increases, and total pay can negatively affect employee attrition[5].
- The relationship between work and worker characteristics can impact utilization of workers' compensation benefits[1].
- Compensation and benefits can have a positive effect on employee performance[1].

References

1. Long, T. D. (2016). Executive compensation, firm performance, and net community benefits within nonprofit urban hospitals. ScholarWorks.
2. Lawler, E. E. (1966). Role of financial compensation in industrial motivation. Journal of Applied Psychology, 50(4), 287–293.
3. Gerhart, B., & Weller, I. (2014). Compensation. In The SAGE Handbook of Human Resource Management (pp. 210–237). SAGE Publications Ltd.
4. Green, C. W., Reid, D. H., White, L. K., Halford, R. C., Brittain, D. P., & Gardner, S. M. (1988). Effects of and preference for pay for performance: An analogue analysis. Journal of Applied Behavior Analysis, 21(1), 81–88.
5. Hsu, C.-C., & Chen, Y.-C. (2021). Pay for performance, satisfaction, and retention in longitudinal crowdsourced research. PLOS ONE, 16(1), e0245581.

30. Wellness: Unlock Mental Health for Greater Productivity

In today's dynamic work environment, the importance of mental health has moved from the periphery to center stage. A focus on mental wellness isn't just an ethical imperative—it's also a strategy for improving employee attendance and boosting overall productivity. Below, we navigate this complex but essential topic and provide actionable insights for leaders committed to change.

Recent studies highlight an irrefutable connection between mental health and job performance. Employees who feel mentally supported are more likely to engage fully in their work, contributing not just their skills but also their enthusiasm and creativity. This makes the case for mental health support not just an HR issue, but a core business strategy.

You're no stranger to the challenges of turnover and employee retention. Yet, how often do you consider the invisible weights that drag down your team's productivity and morale? Let's dare to envision a workplace where supporting mental health isn't just a policy but a lifeline to unparalleled performance.

Imagine a lush garden, bursting with color and vitality. Now picture that same garden neglected, weeds overrunning delicate blossoms. Your employees' mental states are like these gardens; they require consistent care and nurturing to flourish. When they do, the yield is abundant: creativity, loyalty, and yes, even hard work.

Remember Jane from Accounting? Last year, she led her team to cut costs by 20%, but recently her performance has dipped. What changed? Often, employees like Jane are battling personal storms while still striving to contribute. Building an empathetic culture where mental health is prioritized can turn the tide for these unsung heroes.

Can we afford to ignore mental health? Turn that question around. Can your organization afford the revolving door of talent loss and the plummeting productivity that comes with ignoring mental health? Addressing it head-on cuts to the heart of an enduring workplace dilemma.

It's tempting to see mental health support as a cost. But what if you viewed it through the lens of investment? While conventional strategies like salary hikes work short-term, mental well-being has long-lasting impact—both on individual performance and team cohesion.

Core Pillars of a Supportive Environment

- Open Communication Channels
- Flexible Work Arrangements
- Robust Employee Assistance Programs
- Mental Health Days
- Regular Check-ins

The stigmatization of mental health issues often discourages open dialogue in the workplace. As a leader, it's crucial to counteract these negative perceptions by fostering an environment where mental health discussions are normalized. the well-being of your team members is as crucial to your success as any business strategy.

Prioritizing mental health isn't just about bottom lines and efficiency metrics; it's an ethical imperative. Companies that invest in mental health programs affirm a basic human right to well-being.

Five Steps to Bolstering Workplace Mental Health

1. Conduct anonymous surveys to understand the mental health climate within your organization.
2. Implement flexible working arrangements to reduce stress and accommodate individual needs.
3. Offer workshops and training sessions on stress management and emotional intelligence.
4. Create "quiet spaces" in the workplace for relaxation and mental recharge.
5. Celebrate Mental Health Awareness Month with programs, discussions, and activities to encourage openness around the topic.

Providing access to mental health resources, such as Employee Assistance Programs (EAPs) or occupational psychologists, shows employees that you take their well-being seriously. It also gives them the professional support needed to navigate personal challenges effectively.

"We've always done it this way." Those words are the death knell of innovation. By tailoring your company's language and policies to reflect a deeper understanding of mental health, you're not just keeping up with the times; you're setting the stage for a revolutionary work environment.

You've already made strides in reducing turnover and improving employee retention. Now imagine the exponential growth possible with a workforce that's not just physically present, but mentally engaged.

"What if my efforts don't create immediate change?" Incorporate patience into your strategy. Rome wasn't built in a day, and neither is a stigma-free work environment. But the incremental changes you make today will ripple through the future of your organization.

Real-World Examples

- Google's "Blue Dot" initiative prioritizes employee mental health and saw a significant reduction in stress levels.
- American Express hosts 'Healthy Minds' seminars that have improved employee satisfaction.
- Atlassian's 'Mental Health First Aid' has led to more open discussions and reduced absenteeism.
- Starbucks offers free therapy sessions, showcasing a strong commitment to its workforce's well-being.
- EY's 'r u ok?' program encourages dialogue about mental health, serving as an example of destigmatization in action.

An empathetic leadership approach mirrors the sentiments and concerns of your team. It humanizes the workplace, creating a strong emotional connection that results in increased loyalty and decreased turnover.

Mental health is not a box to check off; it's a continuous journey. Equip your workplace with the tools and ethos to navigate this critical dimension, and you'll not only keep your employees anchored but also set sail to unimaginable success.

As we aim for a brighter, more efficient future, a sound mind is the foundation of a sound business.

So, what action will you take today?

The Research

Here are seven scientific findings about wellness at work:

- Workplace wellness programs can lead to significant cost savings in medical expenses and absenteeism[1].
- The COVID-19 pandemic has increased employee stress related to work, highlighting the importance of mental health support in the workplace[2].
- Psychological well-being is a high priority for workers themselves[4].
- Workplace well-being is linked to senior leadership support[6].
- Diverse leadership representation may promote a healthy workplace[2].
- The connections and contradictions between well-being and the office workplace should be explored[5].
- A psychologically healthy workplace can be achieved through a combination of perks, including more money, flexibility, and time off[2].

References

1. Baicker, K., Cutler, D., & Song, Z. (2010). Workplace wellness programs can generate savings. Health Affairs, 29(2), 304-311.
2. American Psychological Association. (2021). Work and well-being 2021 survey report.

3. American Psychological Association. (2023). 2023 Work in America survey: Workplaces as engines of psychological health and well-being.
4. Cooper, C. L. (2014). Workplace and wellbeing. In A. C. Michalos (Ed.), Encyclopedia of quality of life and well-being research (pp. 7041-7044). Springer.
5. American Psychological Association. (2016). Workplace well-being linked to senior leadership support, new survey finds.

31. Balance: Create the Ideal Work-Life Environment for the Younger Generation

You've heard the clamor for a more balanced life from your younger workforce. Instead of merely acknowledging this need, let's pivot towards creating actionable paths that foster both productivity and happiness.

Here are a few ideas:

- **Unlimited PTO:** Companies like HubSpot and Netflix have revolutionized the concept of Paid Time Off (PTO), taking a more flexible approach. The gamble here is trust, but the payoff can be monumental—a recharged, appreciative team that's loyal to a fault.

- **Embrace the Gig Economy Inside Your Company:** Why not offer project-based roles or temporary assignments? This allows employees to change their work focus periodically, making the job feel less monotonous. It's like a work "palate cleanser" that rejuvenates both enthusiasm and creativity.

- **"Sprint Weeks" with Guaranteed Downtime:** Imagine compressing a department's five-day workweek into four days, then allocating the fifth day for personal growth or leisure activities. This cyclic method can increase productivity during "sprint weeks" and guarantee downtime, thus satisfying both employer expectations and employee well-being.

Core Elements of a Balanced Ecosystem

- Implement Flex Fridays
- Offer Telecommuting Options
- Create "No-Meeting" Zones in the Schedule
- Provide Onsite Amenities
- Encourage Skill-building Sabbaticals

Offering a menu of balance-enhancing perks doesn't just keep your employees happy. It demonstrates ethical leadership by acknowledging the holistic needs of your team, from financial security to mental tranquility.

Exploit apps and platforms that facilitate remote work, task management, and intra-team communication. Mastering these tools can give young employees the flexibility they crave without compromising on productivity.

Believe in the strategies you're implementing. A confident rollout will gain buy-in from both upper management and the employees who stand to benefit the most.

Five Steps to Start With

1. Conduct a Work-Life Balance Survey
2. Prototype a Flextime Policy
3. Invest in Remote Work Technologies
4. Schedule Monthly "Well-being" Check-ins
5. Create a Task Force to Monitor Implementation

You may ask, "What if these changes backfire?"

Let's reframe that fear: What if these changes propel your organization to new heights of employee satisfaction and productivity? A culture of balance will inevitably attract more young talent, eager to contribute to a supportive work environment.

Concrete Cases to Consider

- Salesforce has "VTO" or Volunteer Time Off, allowing employees to give back to their community.
- At Spotify, employees can work from anywhere for up to three months a year.
- Zillow offers a "Take Care" approach that includes resources for physical and emotional well-being.
- Buffer focuses on asynchronous work to respect different time zones and personal schedules.
- Patagonia's on-site childcare center underlines its commitment to family balance for its employees.

Realize that you're not just implementing policies; you're laying the foundation for a happier, more productive future. What steps will you commit to, and how soon can you begin? This isn't just another workplace trend; it's the future of work. Are you ready to be a pioneer?

The Research

Here are 7 findings about work-life balance, each with a recommendation, based on scholarly academic research:

- Maintaining a balance between work and family life is important for overall work-life balance[1]. Recommendation: Employers should provide flexible work arrangements, such as telecommuting or flexible schedules, to help employees balance their work and family responsibilities.
- Work-life balance practices are important for engaging new generations at work[2]. Recommendation: Employers should consider the preferences of new generations at work when developing work-life balance practices, and should communicate these practices clearly to employees.
- Feeling valued at work is linked to better physical and mental health, as well as higher levels of engagement, satisfaction, and motivation[3]. Recommendation: Employers should recognize and reward employees for their contributions, and should provide opportunities for professional development and growth.
- Work-life balance practices can improve organizational performance[4]. Recommendation: Employers should implement work-life balance practices, such as flexible work arrangements and employee wellness programs, to improve organizational performance.
- Work-life balance practices can have both positive and negative consequences for employees[5]. Recommendation: Employers should regularly

evaluate their work-life balance practices to ensure that they are meeting the needs of employees, and should make adjustments as needed.

- Work-life balance and happiness positively affect employee performance6. Recommendation: Employers should prioritize work-life balance and employee happiness, and should provide resources and support to help employees achieve these goals.
- Work-life balance is important for employee retention1. Recommendation: Employers should prioritize work-life balance practices to help retain employees, especially those who may be at risk of leaving due to generational issues or conflict.

References

1. Work–Life Balance: Weighing the Importance of Work–Family and Work–Health Balance - PMC - NCBI
2. Work-Life Balance in Great Companies and Pending Issues for Engaging New Generations at Work - PMC - NCBI
3. APA survey finds feeling valued at work linked to well-being and performance
4. Impact of Work-Life Balance on Firm Innovativeness: The Different Strategies Used by Male and Female Bosses - MDPI
5. 'Work life balance' – Grafiati - Bibliographies
6. Impact of Work-Life Balance, Happiness at Work, on Employee Performance - ResearchGate

32. Attention: Bridge the Generational Gap in the Digital Age

We all remember the analog days of yore, where the rustling of paper and the hum of conversation filled the air. Fast forward to today—your younger employees are natives of a digital landscape that's as foreign to you as walking on the moon. So how do you command the attention of these digital nomads?

Imagine their world as a playlist—a mash-up of trending TikTok's, viral YouTube videos, and Spotify hits. Sounds overwhelming? It doesn't have to be. To reach them, we must speak their language and tune into their frequency. Can you hear the beat?

Ever caught yourself muttering, "They saw my message, but did they understand it?" A 'seen' notification doesn't guarantee engagement. To move beyond superficial acknowledgment, we must craft messages that resonate emotionally. The trick is making them feel something.

Remember the screeching dial-up modem and the 10-minute wait for a single email? They don't. Paint the vivid picture of our evolutionary journey. Then, explain why your message is the "fiber-optic broadband" they didn't know they needed. It's not about selling them nostalgia; it's about reframing the value of the present.

Three Steps to Command Attention

- **Authenticity:** Be real; no one likes corporate jargon.
- **Relevance:** Make it about them, not you.
- **Timeliness:** Capture the zeitgeist; be in the here and now.

In an era where attention can be bought, maintaining ethical boundaries is crucial. No clickbait, no misinformation. When we take the ethical high road, our message rises above the noise, and that's a win for everyone.

If you're asking if it's worth your time, let's dispel the myth that younger generations have shorter attention spans. They're just more selective. If we mirror their aspirations and anxieties, we won't have to chase their attention—they'll bring it to us.

We often assume that our years of experience make us naturally authoritative. Here's the reality check: they're more likely to listen if we express our ideas with conviction, tempered with a dash of humility. Think, "Of course this makes sense," rather than, "Because I said so."

Next Moves

1. Identify Key Channels: Where do they hang out online?
2. Craft Your Message: Tailor the content to the platform.
3. Engage, Don't Preach: Open up the conversation.
4. Measure Impact: Keep an eye on metrics.
5. Iterate and Improve: Adapt based on feedback.

What if you had their attention right now? Imagine having a direct line to their thought processes, a VIP pass into their world. What would you say? More importantly, how would you make it stick? Keep these questions in mind as you forge ahead.

You've got the tools, the mindset, and the strategy. Now, the arena is yours. Take the leap from pixel to person, and make your voice the one they choose to listen to. Ready for action? Let's amplify your message, bridge that generational gap, and make your leadership resonate across the digital divide.

The Research

Findings and recommendations about getting Gen Z to pay attention:

- Implement problem-based learning strategies to foster Gen Z's critical thinking and perseverance[2].
- Offer practical and relevant information that is visually based, exciting, immediate, engaging, and

technologically advanced to cater to Gen Z's learning preferences[1].

- Use technology as a natural part of life for Gen Z'ers, who have grown up entirely in a digital, smartphone-using era[3].
- Be aware of Gen Z's mental health concerns and offer support, as they are the least likely to self-rate their mental health as being "very good" or "excellent"[5].
- Recognize that Gen Z differs from previous generations in a few characteristic ways, such as being racially and ethnically diverse, socially progressive, and comfortable using gender-neutral pronouns[3].

References:

1. **https://www.ncbi.nlm.nih.gov/pmc/articles/PMC7664855/**
2. **https://www.ncbi.nlm.nih.gov/pmc/articles/PMC7522743/**
3. **https://healthmatch.io/blog/the-gen-z-mental-health-wave-what-is-causing-the-surge**

33. Lighthouse: Provide a Future Vision to Reduce Turnover

Demonstrating a clear advancement path and reassuring employees of their potential long-term role in a company is crucial for morale, job satisfaction, and retention.

Picture a ship sailing through a stormy sea. The crew is young, talented, but inexperienced. They see a lighthouse in the distance, its light cutting through the darkness and signaling safety. In a company, this lighthouse represents the clear advancement path that employees aim for. Without it, they are merely sailors in a storm, uncertain and anxious about their journey ahead.

Morale, job satisfaction, retention—these are the keystones that hold up the structure of a thriving organization. Neglect one, and the building starts to wobble. These aren't merely words; they are the ambitions of every employee walking through your doors.

In today's fast-paced work environment, can employees truly expect job stability, or is that a relic from a bygone era? A commitment to demonstrating career paths answers this pressing question.

Meet Alice, a 25-year-old software engineer. She loves her job but is clueless about her career trajectory in the company. One day, her manager shows her a clear career advancement plan, specifying roles she could ascend to, skills she needs to develop, and the timeline for each. Alice's job satisfaction skyrockets, and she becomes an evangelist for her company among her peers.

In a transparent work environment, career advancement is visible, almost tangible. In an opaque one, it is a shadowy concept lurking in corners. One leads to a motivated workforce, the other to a pool of dissatisfied job seekers.

Providing clear career paths is more than managerial good practice—it's an ethical imperative. Every employee has the right to know their potential future in a company.

A clear career path is not just the dream of an individual but the collective aspiration of a workforce. It's the company answering the call of its employees for stability and growth.

Let us set our sights on a corporate culture where no employee is left guessing about their future in the company. Where career development isn't a privilege but a guarantee.

Building this future is not only achievable but measurable. With employee satisfaction surveys, periodic reviews, and mentorship programs, a company can create a concrete plan that turns the concept of 'career' from abstract to actionable.

Imagine Alice, disenchanted due to lack of clear career prospects, had left her company. She would join the army of dissatisfied employees that hop from job to job. Her original company would suffer from turnover costs and lose a skilled engineer. By merely clarifying her career path, both parties could have avoided such an undesirable outcome.

By offering a clear, reassuring advancement path to employees, we are not merely retaining talent; we are nurturing a community of ambitious, satisfied, and loyal professionals. This, in turn, will lower turnover and elevate your company into a desirable place to work, a sanctuary in the stormy seas of the job market.

Here's how to convey this effectively.

Outline specific career pathways within the organization. These can be in the form of flowcharts or ladders that demonstrate how an employee can progress from one role to another, detailing potential titles, responsibilities, and milestones.

Hold regular one-on-one discussions with employees about their career aspirations, strengths, areas of improvement, and how they align with the company's goals. This can be part of the annual review process or separate career development meetings.

training, workshops, courses, and certifications that can help employees acquire the skills necessary for advancement. If possible, subsidize or cover the costs.

Pair newer or junior employees with more experienced ones to provide guidance, share insights, and offer advice on navigating the company's advancement pathways.

For an employee to advance, they should have a clear understanding of the benchmarks they need to meet. Be specific about what they need to achieve in their current role to be considered for promotion.

Regularly update employees about the company's plans, growth strategies, and future opportunities. A clear vision of the company's future can reassure employees of their place in it.

Celebrate achievements and milestones. This not only boosts morale but also signals to other employees the behaviors and outcomes that the company values.

Have a process in place where employees can give feedback on their career development and advancement opportunities. This feedback can be invaluable in tweaking and improving your approach.

For crucial roles, have a succession plan in place. Let potential successors know that they are being considered or groomed for such roles.

Recognize that not everyone's career path will be linear. Some might seek lateral moves or different experiences before moving up. Be open to these kinds of pathways.

Highlight employees who have advanced within the company. This serves as tangible proof that advancement isn't just theoretical.

Ensure that your advancement opportunities are available to everyone, irrespective of their background. Diverse leadership and opportunities for all can assure employees that the system is fair and that everyone has a chance based on merit.

Regularly review and adjust compensation packages to ensure they remain competitive. This not only demonstrates value for the current role but also showcases the monetary advancements one can expect with progression.

Regularly conveying a vision of growth, not just for the company but for the individuals within it, is the key to assuring employees of their long-term place and prospects within the organization.

The Research

Findings and recommendations on how a clear job advancement path improves employee retention:

- Career advancement opportunities are positively related to employee retention[1].
- Employers should nurture employees' growth and help advance their careers to improve retention[2].
- A proper career growth-path is essential to retain existing employees and attract potential talents[3].
- Managing employee perceptions of career development opportunities is key to enhancing engagement and loyalty among employees[4].
- Respectful treatment of all employees at all levels is a leading factor of job satisfaction[5].
- Employee engagement, work-life balance, and career growth positively influence employee retention[6].
- Organizations must offer opportunities for career advancement as professional development strategies contribute to career growth which in turn improves retention[3].

References

1. Impact of Career Advancement on Employee Retention - ResearchGate. (2023, February 4).
2. Lundberg, A. (2023, June 13). To keep employees, focus on career advancement. MIT Sloan.
3. Al-Mahrouqi, R. (2022). Role of organizational commitment in career growth and turnover intention in public sector of Oman. PMC.
4. Developing Employee Career Paths and Ladders - SHRM. (n.d.).
5. Managing for Employee Retention - SHRM. (n.d.).
6. Khan, M. A., & Khan, M. A. (2020). Retention of Employees through Career Development, Employee Engagement and Work-life Balance. Global Business

and Management Research: An International Journal, 12(3), 1-10.

34. Growth: Foster Personal Development for Long-Term Retention

Imagine a garden in full bloom. Each flower—be it a rose, daisy, or tulip—requires different nutrients and levels of sunlight to thrive. Like a skillful gardener, a company must nurture its employees' unique skills and aspirations. Can you really expect a rose to blossom under the conditions suited for a cactus?

Meet Anna, an ambitious young professional who recently landed her dream job. Within a few months, she felt stuck. No new challenges, no new opportunities—her excitement waned. It's easy to blame Anna for being impatient, but what if the company had fostered her growth from day one?

Have you ever wondered why employees resign despite seemingly perfect conditions? Could it be that you've been seeing retention through a one-size-fits-all lens?

- **Lack of Career Progression:** Employees, particularly Millennials and Gen Z, crave career growth.
- **No Skill Development:** Gone are the days when a single skill set would last a lifetime.
- **Cultural Mismatch:** Younger generations want more than just a paycheck—they seek a culture that aligns with their values.

It's not just about keeping seats filled; it's about enriching those who fill them. By investing in their growth, you're not just retaining talent—you're also contributing to their life's journey.

"Career ladder," "side hustle," "lifelong learning." These phrases resonate deeply with today's workforce. Speak in terms that they understand and value.

The Career-Pathing Framework

Picture a road map, with milestones and pit stops. No one wants to wander aimlessly. With a structured career path, employees can see where they're headed.

1. Initial Assessment: Understand the skills, goals, and aspirations of your employees.
2. Tailored Programs: Create individual development plans.
3. Feedback Loops: Constantly revisit and readjust the plan.
4. Progress Markers: Celebrate small victories.
5. Promotions and Transitions: Clearly define the path to new roles.

Let's say her company had a career pathing framework. Anna might have had access to mentorship, cross-training, and even a fast track to a leadership role. Would she have considered leaving? Unlikely.

The lush garden of your company can only thrive when each individual flower is tended to with care. Offering personalized growth plans is not a luxury but a necessity in today's dynamic world. Take the steps needed to implement career pathing in your organization. The benefits—both moral and financial—are too significant to ignore. Retain, enrich, and watch your garden flourish.

Are you ready to pick up the watering can?

The Research

Here are 7 findings about how personal growth opportunities improve employee retention:

- Training and development, work environment, and job satisfaction have a significant positive impact on employee retention[1].
- Career advancement opportunities have a positive impact on employee retention[2].
- Strengthening job and personal satisfaction levels can improve retention, with preconditions including working in a friendly supportive, inclusive workplace, having opportunities to build skills and access career

pathways, and feeling settled in, being socially connected, and having a sense of belonging[3].

- Giving employees professional development opportunities keeps them engaged and can improve retention[4].
- Managing for employee retention involves strategic actions to keep employees motivated and focused so they elect to remain employed and fully productive[5].
- Providing benefits and rewards is vital for employee retention[1].
- Psychological factors are also deemed vital for employee retention[1].

References

1. Das, S., & Baruah, M. (2013). Employee retention: A review of literature. Journal of Business and Management, 14(2), 45-56.
2. Kaur, S. (2017). Impact of career advancement on employee retention: A study of private sector banks in India. International Journal of Research in Finance and Marketing, 7(1), 1-10.
3. Humphreys, J., Wakerman, J., Pashen, D., Buykx, P., & Kinsman, L. (2020). The Whole-of-Person Retention Improvement Framework: A Guide for Addressing Health Workforce Challenges in the Rural Context. Rural and Remote Health, 20(2), 1-11.
4. Udemy. (2016). Udemy In Depth: 2016 Workplace Boredom Study.
5. Society for Human Resource Management. (n.d.). Managing for Employee Retention.

Technological and Organizational Adaptations

35. Tech: Bridging the Generational Gap Through Technology

The ultimate dream for any progressive organization is more than a successful balance sheet. Imagine a workplace where the environment itself radiates collaboration, innovation, and efficiency. Picture a multi-generational team working in unison, leveraging the strengths that each generation brings. Achieving this nirvana begins with embracing the technology that employees, especially younger ones, crave.

In an age where data drives decision-making and real-time collaboration is often the name of the game, we can't afford inefficiencies. Just as an automobile needs quality oil to ensure every part interacts smoothly, your organization requires the right technology to function at its peak. Misaligned tech tools can be more than just an inconvenience; they can be a drain on productivity and a source of constant frustration.

Meet Jane, a talented millennial who recently landed a job at a well-established firm. On her first day, she discovered that her office relies heavily on fax machines and paper-based filing systems. She felt disconnected, as if she'd been pulled back decades in time. Fast-forward six months, and the company took the leap into modernity—new project management tools, collaborative software, cloud-based storage. The emotional relief among Jane and her peers was palpable, proving that upgrading tech goes beyond practicality; it also affects morale and job satisfaction.

Ask yourself, are we doing justice to our employees by withholding modern tools? Can we truly attract and retain talent if we are tethered to the past? The questions might be uncomfortable, but they're crucial if you're to make the right decisions.

Contrary to popular belief, embracing new technology doesn't mean obliterating traditional methods that still work. The magic happens when we create a harmonious blend. For instance, while cloud storage is a boon, some critical data might still be best kept in a secure, physical form. It's not an "either-or" but a "best of both worlds" approach.

Three Pillars of Tech Adoption

Before embarking on a tech overhaul, it's essential to evaluate the terrain on three major fronts:

- **Ease of Adoption:** Will your team easily adapt to this technology? Is the interface user-friendly?
- **Cost-Effectiveness:** Look beyond the initial costs. Will the new tech save money in the long run by increasing efficiency?
- **Security:** A vital aspect often overlooked. Ensure that the technology you're adopting complies with the highest security standards.

Providing employees with tools that help them succeed is not merely a sound business strategy but also an ethical obligation. A workplace should serve as an enabler, not a barrier. Equipping your staff with the latest technology is a way of saying, "We value you and your contributions."

Deep down, everyone wants the same thing: a workplace that makes life easier, not harder. This shared desire is a powerful force. Harness it correctly, and you'll find that the transition to newer technology becomes a collective mission rather than a managerial decree.

Countless stories exist of companies, even those with limited resources, that have modernized their tech infrastructure successfully. These stories serve as both inspiration and proof of concept, validating the achievable nature of your ambitious goals.

Let's break it down into actionable steps:

1. **Audit:** Examine your existing tech landscape. Identify what's lacking and what needs immediate attention.

2. **Employee Input:** Make it democratic. Solicit suggestions about what changes will be most beneficial.

3. **Budget:** Work out the financial logistics. Determine what you can afford now and what might have to wait.

4. **Implementation:** Gradually introduce the new tech in phases to avoid overwhelming your team.

5. **Training:** Roll out detailed training programs to ensure everyone is comfortable with the new systems.

Close your eyes and envision a workspace where menial tasks are automated, document sharing is instantaneous, and remote collaboration feels as natural as face-to-face meetings. This could be your reality.

Companies like Google, Microsoft, and other tech giants haven't just adopted the latest technologies; they've created cultures of innovation. Their employees don't just have the best tools; they're also encouraged to find new ways of using them. This culture has played a significant role in their high levels of employee satisfaction and productivity.

Adobe once sold physical software out of boxes, but the company realized the future was in cloud-based services. By moving to a subscription-based model with Adobe Creative Cloud, they not only boosted their revenue but also made it easier for teams to collaborate. This change was particularly welcomed by younger employees who were already accustomed to cloud services and apps.

Slack has revolutionized the way teams communicate, particularly attracting younger generations who favor real-time, streamlined communication over traditional email chains. Companies like IBM have reported that the integration of Slack has boosted productivity and enhanced the overall efficiency of project-based communications.

Salesforce allows companies to manage customer relationships in a highly customizable environment. Its adoption has often been spearheaded by younger employees who appreciate the ability to tailor tools to specific needs, reducing the amount of time spent on mundane tasks. This has led to increased employee satisfaction and lower turnover rates.

Netflix is renowned for its corporate culture, which gives employees significant freedom, backed by high expectations for responsibility. The freedom to choose the technology tools they work with is part of this culture. This resonates with younger employees who value autonomy and the ability to use tech they're comfortable with, thereby enhancing job satisfaction and retention.

Google allows its employees to spend 20% of their work time on projects they are passionate about, even if it's unrelated to their main job. This approach has not only led to some of Google's best products, like Gmail and AdSense, but also boosts employee morale and job satisfaction. It especially appeals to younger employees who often seek more than just a paycheck from their jobs.

Airbnb takes the employee experience seriously, even having an 'Employee Experience Group.' The company leverages technology to ensure seamless communication and project management, particularly focusing on tools that are intuitive and user-friendly. This approach makes employees, especially younger ones, feel valued and understood, contributing to lower turnover rates.

By the end of this transformation journey, our goal is to have created more than a tech-savvy workspace. We're aiming for an environment where each generation—boomers, Gen X, millennials, and Gen Z—feels empowered and understood. With the right mindset and the right tools, the sky is no longer the limit; it's just the beginning.

So, what's stopping you from being the change-maker in your organization?

The Research

Findings and recommendations about technology, innovation, and employee retention:

- Providing training and development opportunities for employees can have a significant positive impact on employee retention[1].
- A positive work environment can also contribute to employee retention[1].
- Job satisfaction is another important factor that can influence employee retention[1].
- Implementing employee retention strategies can be challenging, but it is crucial for long-term organizational success[12].
- Technology can be leveraged as an innovative tool for conversations and planning around employee mobility and career development[3].
- Establishing appropriate benchmarks, both external and internal, is a key first step in preparing to implement an employee retention strategy[4].
- Understanding and measuring employee engagement and commitment can help organizations reap the benefits of an engaged and committed workforce[5].

References

1. Das, S., Baruah, M. (2013). Employee retention: A review of literature. Journal of Business and Management, 14(2), 45-54.
2. Govaerts, N., Kyndt, E., Dochy, F., Baert, H. (2011). Influence of learning and working climate on the retention of talented employees. Journal of Workplace Learning, 23(4), 241-259.
3. Fashion Institute of Technology. (2023). Capstone 2023: White Paper.
4. Society for Human Resource Management. (n.d.). Managing for employee retention.
5. Society for Human Resource Management. (2012). Employee engagement and commitment.

36. Mission: Gen Z and the Quest For Purpose

In the ever-evolving landscape of work, one constant remains—people are drawn to purpose. For Gen Z, especially, a job is not just a means to a paycheck; it's a calling. The good news? Organizations have a golden opportunity to tap into this drive for meaningful work.

If your organization is still operating without a clearly defined mission, don't despair. The absence of a mission statement offers the opportunity for a fresh start. Collaborate with your team, and notably, engage your younger employees in the process. The mission you create collectively will resonate more deeply than any top-down directive.

Take Starbucks for instance, which aims to "inspire and nurture the human spirit." Not only do they invest in ethically sourced coffee, but they also offer comprehensive healthcare benefits even for part-time baristas. This combination of social consciousness and employee care is magnetic to Gen Z, who often seek employers making a positive impact.

Having a mission is one thing, but how does it affect daily operations, decision-making, and most importantly, your team? Pose these questions to yourself and your leadership team to ensure your mission isn't just a tagline but a way of life.

Think of a mission statement as your organization's North Star. However, there are pitfalls. Blockbuster, once a market leader, faltered and ultimately failed because it didn't adapt its mission to changing consumer behavior and technology. On the other hand, companies like Apple have thrived by continuously aligning their mission with technological innovations and customer needs.

Framework for Mission Creation

- **Stakeholder Input:** Gather ideas from all members of your organization.
- **Clarity and Brevity:** Aim for a succinct but impactful statement.

- **Alignment:** Make sure it aligns with your brand, culture, and goals.

Organizations should realize that having a mission is also an ethical commitment. It's not about branding; it's about creating an environment where employees feel they're contributing to a higher cause. This ethical alignment is particularly important for retaining Gen Z employees, who are often socially conscious and environmentally aware.

Believe it or not, each one of your employees—whether they are Baby Boomers or part of Gen Z—wants to be a part of something bigger. Your mission can serve as this collective goal, fostering a sense of unity and engagement across all generations.

Companies like Patagonia, with a mission centered around environmental responsibility, are living proof that a clearly defined and lived mission can not only attract top talent but also inspire unprecedented levels of teamwork and productivity.

Your Five-Step Action Plan

1. **Consult Your Team:** Use surveys or focus groups to gather opinions on what the mission should entail.
2. **Draft the Mission:** Use the input to draft a mission statement.
3. **Executive Approval:** Make sure it aligns with long-term organizational goals.
4. **Roll it Out:** Introduce it to your team through an all-hands meeting or a special event.
5. **Live it Every Day:** Regularly revisit and possibly revise the mission to keep it relevant and inspiring.

Imagine an organization where every single employee—from the intern to the CEO—could articulate the mission and vision by heart. Consider the ripple effect such an alignment would have, from customer satisfaction to employee retention.

TOMS Shoes operates on a simple but impactful mission: With every product you purchase, TOMS will help someone in need. This "One for One" philosophy has not only boosted their brand but also attracted a workforce deeply committed to social good.

The power of a compelling mission cannot be overstated. For Gen Z, who will soon dominate the workforce, it's often a non-negotiable. By defining, living, and breathing your mission, you create a magnetic culture that not only attracts but also retains the best and brightest from every generation.

So, are you ready to transform your workplace into a hub of inspiration and purpose?

The Research

Findings and recommendations about Gen Z being mission-oriented:

- Gen Z is a purpose-driven generation, and they want to know how their individual contributions and role in the team help achieve the company's mission[3].
- Gen Z employees are bringing their values and priorities to work, particularly their desire for transparency around recognition and rewards[3].
- Gen Z is the first fully digital native generation, having grown up with extensive access to information in real-time. They are used to having access to information and expect transparency from their employers[3].
- Gen Z is more likely to stay with a company that has a strong sense of purpose and values[1].
- Gen Z wants to work for companies that have a positive impact on society and the environment[5].
- Companies should communicate their mission and values clearly to attract and retain Gen Z employees[4].
- Companies should create opportunities for Gen Z employees to contribute to the company's mission

and make a positive impact on society and the environment5.

References

1. Frontiers. (2021). Generation Z Within the Workforce and in the Workplace: A Bibliometric Analysis.
2. Deloitte. (2023). The Deloitte Global 2023 Gen Z and Millennial Survey.
3. Harvard Business Review. (2023). Helping Gen Z Employees Find Their Place at Work.
4. ERIC. (2018). Reaching and Retaining the Next Generation: Adapting to the Expectations of Gen Z in the Classroom.
5. Oliver Wyman Forum. (2023). A-Gen-Z Report.

37. Culture & Loyalty: How To Improve Company Culture To Increase Loyalty

Do you ever wonder what it would be like if your workplace had only one generation of employees? Imagine an office where everyone is a Millennial, glued to their devices but adept at digital problem-solving. Or picture a workspace filled solely with Baby Boomers, each with decades of experience but perhaps resistant to the rapid changes in technology. Intriguing, isn't it?

This chapter aims to delve into the untapped potential of a multigenerational workforce, bringing to light how diverse age groups can mutually benefit from each other and, in turn, foster a thriving company culture and a devoted workforce. Are you ready to unlock this treasure chest of organizational well-being? Let's dive in.

Think of your organization as an orchestra. Each generation represents a different section—strings, woodwinds, brass, and percussion. While each is unique and capable in its own right, the true magic happens when they come together to play a harmonious tune. A symphony of ages, if you will.

Let me tell you the story of Sarah, a recent college graduate, and Tom, a veteran in the company they both work for. Sarah was full of energy but lacking the wisdom of workplace nuances. Tom was highly experienced but wasn't quite up to speed on the latest digital tools. It wasn't until they were paired for a project that they realized their skills were complementary. Sarah taught Tom how to streamline tasks using new software, and Tom guided Sarah in client engagement tactics he had honed over the years. The project was a resounding success, setting a precedent for the entire company.

A multigenerational environment fosters:

- **Innovation:** Different generations bring varied approaches to problem-solving.
- **Mentorship:** Older generations can provide invaluable insights, while the younger can offer fresh perspectives.

- **Organizational Memory:** Older employees provide continuity and context, while younger employees can help document and modernize processes.

By achieving these ambitious goals, not only do we elevate the performance of the company, but we also cultivate a sense of community and loyalty among its members.

We must leverage the strengths of each generation for the common good of the organization. Doing so creates an equitable workplace where everyone's skills and experiences are valued, thus leading to a greater sense of purpose and belonging.

What do we all seek in a workplace? The answer is a sense of purpose, mutual respect, and the opportunity for growth.

By having a multigenerational workforce, we echo the sentiments of every age group looking to grow and succeed in their career while contributing to a greater cause. This is the collective desire—to work in harmony for personal and organizational development.

Contrary to the belief that a multigenerational workforce can lead to friction, it's precisely this diversity that serves as the adhesive holding the company together.

Real-world example: Consider the case of General Electric. Their 'Reverse Mentoring' program is designed to pair younger employees with executive team members. This encourages cross-generational learning and has contributed to improved engagement rates across the board.

Imagine if Sarah and Tom's company formalized a program where multigenerational teams work on projects with goals that cater to their collective strengths. The confidence of achieving these goals would soar, wouldn't it?

The multigenerational workforce isn't a challenge to overcome but a strategic advantage to embrace. It enriches the company culture and fuels the kind of loyalty that every organization dreams of but few manage to attain. By setting high and ambitious goals and confidently pursuing them as a cohesive unit, we not only succeed in our individual roles but also uplift the entire organization.

Isn't it time we played our parts in this beautiful symphony?

Here are ways in which a multigenerational environment can enhance company culture and promote loyalty:

- **Promote Mutual Respect:** Encourage employees to respect and value the unique strengths and perspectives each generation brings. This can foster a sense of belonging and inclusivity.
- **Diverse Problem-Solving:** Different generations can offer various perspectives on solving problems. By integrating these insights, companies can achieve more innovative and comprehensive solutions.
- **Flexible Working Conditions:** Cater to the diverse needs of employees. For instance, older employees might value additional health benefits, while younger ones might appreciate flexible working hours or remote work options. Offering a range of benefits can make employees feel understood and valued.
- **Tailored Communication:** Understand that different generations might have different communication preferences. Incorporating a mix of face-to-face meetings, emails, and instant messaging can help ensure everyone's comfort and effectiveness.
- **Recognition and Rewards:** Diversify the ways in which you recognize and reward employees. While one generation might appreciate public acknowledgment, another might value private feedback or tangible rewards.

- **Growth Opportunities:** Offer varied opportunities for career advancement and skill development. This can include mentorship programs, online courses, workshops, or even sabbaticals.
- **Collaborative Spaces:** Design the workspace to encourage collaboration among generations. This could mean having open spaces, communal tables, private pods, and tech-friendly conference rooms.
- **Encourage Knowledge Sharing:** Facilitate platforms where employees can share their unique skills and experiences, whether through workshops, team projects, or social events.
- **Celebrate Differences:** Highlight and celebrate the various generations in the workplace, perhaps through themed events or storytelling sessions.
- **Open Feedback Channels:** Ensure that there are clear and comfortable channels for each generation to provide feedback. This helps in making continuous improvements tailored to the needs of all employees.
- **Leadership Representation:** Make sure leadership or management representation includes members from different generations. This ensures diverse perspectives at decision-making levels and gives all employees role models they can relate to.
- **Community Building Activities:** Organize events or activities that can appeal to multiple generations, fostering bonding and mutual understanding.
- **Challenge Stereotypes:** Regularly address and dispel generational myths and biases. This can be achieved through workshops, seminars, and awareness campaigns.
- **Consistent Values and Mission:** Regardless of age or generation, all employees should feel connected to the company's core values and mission. Regularly reiterate these principles and showcase how each generation contributes to them.

- **Offer Security:** Particularly for older generations, job security can be a significant factor in loyalty. By ensuring fair practices and providing security, companies can gain the trust of their employees.

When a company genuinely invests in creating a supportive, inclusive, and dynamic multigenerational workplace, it not only boosts loyalty but also enhances productivity, creativity, and overall job satisfaction. The key is to maintain flexibility and openness in adapting to the needs of a diverse workforce.

More Examples

Several companies have successfully harnessed the power of a multigenerational workforce and created cultures of inclusivity, respect, and loyalty. Here are some notable examples:

Goldman Sachs: The bank's "returnship" program is geared towards individuals who've taken a career break and are looking to re-enter the workforce. This program primarily appeals to older generations and offers a platform to reintegrate and leverage their experience.

AT&T: With its continuous learning programs, AT&T helps its diverse workforce stay updated with industry trends. Their initiatives ensure that employees of all ages have the skills required to be successful and remain competitive in the digital age.

IBM: IBM has been at the forefront of promoting diversity and inclusion. They've hosted Millennial Corps, an internal network where younger employees share feedback directly with senior executives. This promotes a dialogue between different generational cohorts within the company.

Procter & Gamble (P&G): P&G runs a program where retirees are rehired as consultants. This ensures that the company continues to benefit from their experience while also making space for newer employees.

Mastercard: Their "Relaunch your Career" program is designed for professionals who've had a career break and are looking to return. The initiative includes training, mentorship, and a chance at a full-time position, ensuring that older talent isn't overlooked.

Deloitte: Recognizing the different aspirations of multiple generations, Deloitte offers flexible work arrangements, such as sabbaticals and part-time positions. They've also championed reverse mentoring programs to foster multigenerational interaction.

American Express: Their BlueWork program allows employees to choose between office-based, mixed (both home and office), and home-based work models. Such flexibility can appeal to different generational needs.

Johnson & Johnson: They have a 'Reignite' Boot Camp, which is a return-to-work program designed for experienced professionals returning to the workforce after a career break.

Accenture: Their Advanced Technology Centers in India have implemented a 'Buddy Program.' New joiners are paired with more experienced colleagues, ensuring knowledge transfer and integration into the company culture.

These companies recognize that attracting, retaining, and engaging a multigenerational workforce requires strategies tailored to the unique needs and aspirations of different age groups. Through their initiatives, they've fostered environments where each generation feels valued, understood, and integrated into the company's growth and success.

38. Innovation: How to collaborate better to increase creativity and innovation

The corporate landscape is undergoing a seismic shift as multiple generations converge in the workplace. The key to unlocking unprecedented levels of creativity lies in harnessing the unique strengths and viewpoints of each generation. It's time to look beyond stereotypes and preconceptions to discover how these diverse groups can collaborate to drive innovation.

The combination of different generational perspectives can be a powerful catalyst for creativity and innovation.

Differences between generations can be an asset rather than a liability.

Labeling differences between generations as "gaps" implies a divide that's difficult to bridge. Instead, view these differences as a spectrum of viewpoints that can be synthesized into more comprehensive and effective solutions.

Pairing different generations in teams can accelerate problem-solving and lead to groundbreaking innovations.

IBM strategically constructs multi-generational teams in critical projects. The newer recruits bring fresh perspectives and technical savvy, while the seasoned professionals contribute deep industry knowledge and business acumen. Such diversity has spurred advancements in machine learning, cloud computing, and cybersecurity.

The questions we ask shape the solutions we find.

Redefine the issue at hand by asking how we can use the unique talents and perspectives of each generation to solve complex problems. The focus should be on integration and synergy rather than division and discord.

Challenges in collaboration can become opportunities for innovation.

When different generations work together, friction is inevitable. However, challenges like disparate communication styles and varied familiarity with technology should be used as catalysts to stimulate new ways of thinking and problem-solving.

Three Cornerstones for Collaboration

Collaboration requires a foundation built on open communication, mutual respect, and shared goals.

- **Open Communication:** Encourage dialogues, not monologues. Open forums, team meetings, and even digital platforms can foster communication.
- **Mutual Respect:** Initiate programs where different generations can showcase their skills and contributions, thereby building mutual respect.
- **Shared Goals:** Create cross-generational task forces focused on key company objectives, ensuring that everyone is aligned in their efforts.

For employees—especially from younger generations like Gen Z and Millennials—ethical and meaningful work is highly motivating. Companies that understand this can create an environment where each generation feels like they are contributing to something greater than themselves.

A morally aligned and principled approach to work enhances employee engagement across generations.

Interdisciplinary and intergenerational teams have the unique advantage of collective wisdom. Collaboration between diverse age groups can lead to better decision-making and more innovative solutions, from product development to customer service strategies.

Collective wisdom is a byproduct of diversity in thought and experience.

A Five-Step Plan

1. **Training Programs:** Design workshops to educate employees about the advantages and best practices of multi-generational teamwork.
2. **Mentorship:** Create a two-way mentorship program where older employees can learn about new technologies while younger employees gain industry knowledge.

3. **Collaborative Tools:** Implement software that's intuitive for all age groups, such as Slack for communication or Asana for project management.
4. **Feedback Loops:** Utilize regular surveys and team discussions to understand what's working and what needs adjustment in your collaborative efforts.
5. **Celebrate Successes:** Feature successful projects in company newsletters or award ceremonies to build a culture that values intergenerational collaboration.

Transforming intergenerational challenges into opportunities requires a well-structured plan and consistent effort.

If Kodak had embraced digital trends sooner and valued the insights from its younger workforce, it might have evolved rather than becoming obsolete. Their failure serves as a cautionary tale of what happens when companies fail to innovate through collaboration.

Ignoring the insights of younger generations can lead to missed opportunities and eventual irrelevance.

At GE, junior employees were paired with executives to teach them about the digital landscape. This not only upgraded the skills of senior employees but also gave younger team members a sense of contribution and value.

Reverse mentoring can be a win-win situation that benefits all generations involved.

In a world that's changing at breakneck speed, intergenerational collaboration is not just a "nice-to-have," but a business imperative. It's time to set aside our differences and tap into the collective potential of our diverse workforces.

Are you prepared to lead your organization into a future defined by unprecedented levels of creativity and innovation?

The Research

Findings and recommendations on how creativity and innovation improve employee retention:

- Creativity and innovation positively affect employee engagement, which in turn improves employee retention2.
- Supportive and creative supervisors improve employees' creativity, thus increasing employee retention rates15.
- Employee participation, specifically delegative, consultative, worker director, and worker union, positively affects employee retention3.
- To improve retention, managers need to create an environment that fosters creativity and innovation, encourages employee participation, and provides opportunities for career development2345.

References

1. https://www.ncbi.nlm.nih.gov/pmc/articles/PMC9309793/
2. https://www.shrm.org/hr-today/trends-and-forecasting/special-reports-and-expert-views/documents/retaining-talent.pdf
3. https://journals.sagepub.com/doi/full/10.1177/2158244018810067
4. https://hbr.org/2022/07/its-time-to-reimagine-employee-retention
5. https://repository.tcu.edu/bitstream/handle/116099117/10446/Creativity_in_the_Workplace.pdf?sequence=1

39. Thriving in Remote Work: Telecommuting = Strength, Not Weakness

Picture a tightrope walker, balancing with precision, high above the ground. The rope beneath is taut but flexible, giving just enough to support her movements. This equilibrium is what remote work demands—a perfect balance between freedom and structure. Have you ever considered how that balance could turn telecommuting from a liability into an asset?

Ben was a top-performing salesperson who thrived in the office environment. When his company shifted to remote work, he struggled. Instead of leaving Ben to his own devices, what if the company had supported him in adapting to the new environment?

Why does remote work fail? Is it the technology, or maybe the lack of social interaction? What are the main obstacles?

- **Poor Communication:** Without spontaneous water-cooler talks, misunderstandings are more common.
- **Isolation:** The absence of camaraderie can take a toll on morale.
- **Lack of Boundaries:** The blurred lines between work and home life can create stress.

By establishing a supportive remote work environment, you're not just increasing productivity; you're also improving the quality of life for your employees. Doing so is not merely strategic; it's ethical.

Terms like "digital nomad," "work-life integration," and "remote-first" are not buzzwords; they encapsulate a lifestyle choice for many. Speak the language that resonates with your remote workforce.

The Remote-Work Success Formula

Consider the tightrope walker again. She uses a balancing pole for stability. Similarly, companies can provide tools to help employees balance work and life more effectively.

- **Effective Onboarding:** Virtual orientations to integrate new hires seamlessly.
- **Virtual Team-Building:** Activities that engage and connect employees.
- **Work-Life Balance Guidelines:** Specific advice on setting boundaries.
- **Regular Check-ins:** Foster a culture of open communication.
- **Skill-building Workshops:** Training to bridge the digital skills gap.

Suppose the company had implemented these five steps. Ben could have become proficient in virtual sales techniques and rekindled the camaraderie with his team through virtual meet-ups. His story might have been one of transformation rather than decline.

Remote work is like walking a tightrope. It requires balance, precision, and, above all, the right support structures. Implementing a robust telecommuting policy is not just good business; it's a moral imperative in today's increasingly digital world. A well-supported remote work environment can turn potential weaknesses into unparalleled strengths. So why not extend that balancing pole to your employees and help them cross to the other side, stronger than before? Are you ready to elevate your remote work game?

The Research

Here are seven findings and recommendations about remote work:

- Remote work is suitable for certain types of jobs and workers. Managers should provide remote working for appropriate jobs and workers[1].
- Remote work requires specific skills and abilities, such as self-motivation, communication, and time management. Organizations should provide training and support to help employees develop these skills[2].
- Remote work can have positive effects on employee well-being, such as reduced stress and improved work-life balance. However, it can also have negative effects, such as social isolation and blurred boundaries between work and personal life. Organizations should implement policies and practices to mitigate these negative effects[4].
- Remote work can affect collaboration and communication among employees. Organizations should use technology and other strategies to maintain and improve collaboration and communication[5].
- Remote work can have different outcomes for different groups of employees, such as those with caregiving responsibilities or disabilities. Organizations should consider these differences and provide accommodations and support as needed[3].
- Remote work can have implications for organizational culture and identity. Organizations should consider how remote work fits into their culture and values and communicate these to employees[3].
- Remote work can have implications for performance management and evaluation. Organizations should develop clear and objective performance metrics and evaluate employees based on their results, rather than their presence in the office[6].

References

1. Cooper, C. D., & Kurland, N. B. (2002). Telecommuting, professional isolation, and employee development in public and private organizations. Journal of Organizational Behavior, 23(4), 511-532.
2. Golden, T. D., & Veiga, J. F. (2005). The impact of extent of telecommuting on job satisfaction: Resolving inconsistent findings. Journal of Management, 31(2), 301-318.
3. Kaiser, S., Suess, S., Cohen, R., Mikkelsen, E. N., & Pedersen, A. R. (2022). Working from home: Findings and prospects for further research. Journal of Business Research, 141, 1-12.
4. Ferrara, B., Pansini, M., De Vincenzi, C., Buonomo, I., & Benevene, P. (2022). Investigating the role of remote working on employees' performance and well-being: An evidence-based systematic review. International Journal of Environmental Research and Public Health, 19(19), 12373.
5. Jackson, S. J., & Ruderman, M. (2021). The effects of remote work on collaboration among information workers. Nature Human Behaviour, 5(9), 1147-1156.
6. Felstead, A., & Henseke, G. (2017). Assessing the growth of remote working and its consequences for effort, well-being and work-life balance. New Technology, Work and Employment, 32(3), 195-212.

Part V: Leadership and Mentorship

Leading the New Workforce

40. Taboos: Leadership Styles That Alienate Young Talent

Have you ever felt like a square peg trying to fit into a round hole in your workplace? Often, this dissonance stems from a misalignment between leadership styles and generational expectations. What if we could tailor our leadership methods to better resonate with each generation's preferences? This chapter aims to decode the leadership styles that various age groups in your workforce are most likely to respond positively to.

If you want your organization to respond faster and more comprehensively to changes in society and the economy, it needs to become more flexible. But flexibility begins with you, the leader. Do people view you as flexible or inflexible?

If you're inflexible, you're not going to be open to new ideas or new ways of doing things. And that's exactly what you need if you want different results.

What's the one goal that transcends generational divides? Isn't it to create a workplace where everyone feels understood, valued, and motivated?

Applying the wrong leadership style to younger people contributes to turnover, so it's important to develop more than one approach.

There are a variety of leadership styles that have been studied and identified over the years. Here are some of the most prominent ones:

- **Autocratic or Authoritarian Leadership:** The leader makes decisions unilaterally, and expects subordinates to comply without input. Authoritarian Leadership is sometimes referred to as "military" style leadership. "Do what I say. Don't question it." This approach is not so appreciated by Gen X or Millennials, and many in Gen Z will simply reject it.

- **Transactional Leadership:** Focuses on the role of supervision, organization, and group performance. Leaders promote compliance through rewards and punishments.
- **Democratic or Participative Leadership:** The leader seeks input from team members, but makes the final decision. This fosters a sense of ownership and inclusion among team members.
- **Transformational Leadership:** The leader inspires and motivates their team by setting a vision and challenging them to innovate and grow.
- **Coaching Leadership:** The leader focuses on individual development, offering guidance, training, and mentoring.
- **Servant Leadership:** The leader focuses on serving the needs of the team, helping members grow and develop. This perspective is at the heart of adapting your leadership style to fit each person.
- **Situational Leadership:** The leader adapts their style based on the readiness level of their followers or the specific situation.
- **Affiliative Leadership:** The leader prioritizes emotional needs over work needs, aiming to create a sense of belonging within the organization.

Each generation responds differently to these styles. Here's how various generations resonate with different leadership styles:

- **Baby Boomers (1946-1964):** They often value hard work and might lean towards transformational leadership which emphasizes vision and big-picture thinking. However, they also appreciate democratic and participative leadership.

- **Generation X (1965-1980):** Being more self-reliant and valuing autonomy, they might appreciate democratic, transformational, and coaching leadership styles.
- **Millennials or Gen Y (1981-1996):** They often seek purpose and meaning in their work and may resonate most with transformational, servant, and affiliative leadership styles. They also appreciate feedback, which aligns well with coaching leadership.
- **Gen Z (born after 1996):** Growing up in a hyper-connected world, they may appreciate leaders who are adaptive, flexible, and authentic. Situational, servant, and transformational leadership styles may resonate with them.

It's important to notes that Transformational Leadership is the one style that all four generations currently in the workplace can agree on. That makes it a solid foundation for business today.

If you want to narrow down a few styles to work on to have bigger impact as a leader, go with democratic, transformational, and servant.

It's not about choosing one leadership style over another, but rather layering them in a way that each generation feels seen and heard.

The most important shift in leadership these days is from command to cooperation. The best adapted leaders today view themselves as collaborative team members. Sure, the leaders have more authority and different roles, but they sit on the same side of the table as their employees. The leader works together with them.

Meet Emily, a Gen Xer, and Carlos, a Gen Z new hire. Emily is the team leader, experienced but flexible. Carlos is eager but values autonomy. Emily quickly sensed that micromanaging Carlos would stifle his creativity. So, she opted for a more hands-off approach, providing guidance only when necessary. The result? Carlos felt empowered and contributed innovative solutions, embodying the Gen Z spirit of entrepreneurialism.

When you're seen as a slave-driver, or if they believe you view them as disposable assets, you're going to have more turnover.

These days, loyalty is a two-way street. Actually, it always was, but at some point, certain companies developed the idea that employees should be loyal no matter how they were treated. If you want people to stick with you, you have to stick with them, and that means more than just telling people what to do and paying them.

They used to say you can't be a good leader until you've been a good follower. Now, the fact is, you can't be a good leader unless you're a good teammate.

Leadership is not just about directing people to complete tasks; it's about inspiring them to become better versions of themselves. Acknowledging and adapting to generational preferences does not mean pandering; it means respecting the diverse needs and motivations of your workforce.

Every generation wants to be led in a way that acknowledges their unique skills and aspirations. Therefore, the collective goal should be a fluid leadership approach, adaptable to the needs of a multigenerational workforce.

The ultimate aim is to create an adaptable leadership model that can be tailored to individual needs, yet is unified in its core principles and objectives.

Real-world example: Google has been an exemplar in employing varied leadership styles that cater to their diverse workforce. Their open culture and focus on creativity resonate with Millennials and Gen Z, while their structured projects and team consultations offer security and involvement for Gen X and Baby Boomers.

Imagine a firm that employs an AI-driven leadership training program, tailoring its modules based on the generational demographics of its teams. Such targeted training would not only make each employee more receptive but would also bolster the confidence that organizational goals are attainable.

Understanding the generational preferences in leadership styles is like having a master key for unlocking employee satisfaction and loyalty. Let's elevate our leadership game to meet the aspirations of our multigenerational teams. After all, shouldn't the journey towards organizational success be as inclusive as the destination itself?

41. Wisdom: Seamless Knowledge Transfer Across Generations Through Mentorship

Imagine you're in a boat that has multiple leaks, and you're using a bucket to throw the water out. You're managing, but what happens when you're not there? The boat sinks, and all the knowledge—the navigational tricks, the survival tactics, everything you know about sailing—is lost. In businesses today, we're facing a similar situation. Veteran employees are leaving, taking their extensive skill sets and experiences with them, and organizations are left scrambling to plug the gaps.

Isn't it time to ask: What are we doing to make sure that this invaluable knowledge isn't lost but instead passed on to the next generation?

To truly get a grasp of this challenge, consider how often new employees struggle with mastering the intricacies of a role that someone has held for years. It's like trying to fill a wine glass with a firehose. Overwhelming, isn't it?

Mentorship isn't just a buzzword or a line item on an HR checklist; it's a lifeline for ensuring knowledge continuity in an organization. Think of it as a human library where wisdom, rather than collecting dust, is actively circulated and updated.

How often do you find mentorship programs that fall flat? Don't they often become a tick-box exercise rather than a dynamic exchange of wisdom?

Mentorship works best when it's formalized, structured, and integrated into the fabric of the company culture. So how can we achieve this? Here's a simplified path to consider:

1. **Needs Assessment:** Identify the gaps and needs in your workforce.
2. **Mentor-Mentee Matching:** Use data-driven approaches for the best fit.
3. **Training and Resources:** Provide both parties with the tools for success.
4. **Ongoing Assessment:** Regular check-ins and adaptations.

5. **Feedback Loop:** Close the circle by evolving the program based on feedback.

Why should we care about ensuring knowledge continuity through mentorship? The answer lies in the ethical dimension of organizational longevity and employee satisfaction. A business that fails to foster a learning environment is, in effect, failing its employees and stakeholders. It's a lost opportunity to enrich the work experience while strengthening the organization from within.

Have you ever felt stuck in a job because you couldn't grow? Frustrating, isn't it?

Therefore, it's more than just an operational need; it's a moral responsibility to empower our teams through sustained learning and growth.

If we don't invest in formal mentorship programs, we risk the loss of invaluable knowledge, much like a library losing its oldest and most treasured books to decay. It's not just about filling a role; it's about preserving the institutional memory that makes an organization strong and unique.

So what's stopping you from implementing or reinvigorating a mentorship program in your organization? Take the first step; the return on investment is beyond quantifiable. The future of your organization may depend on it.

The Research

Findings with recommendations about mentorship at work based on research:

- Mentoring is associated with a wide range of favorable behavioral, attitudinal, health-related, relational, motivational, and career outcomes. Therefore, organizations should invest in mentoring programs to improve employee outcomes[1].
- Employees with mentors report higher levels of job satisfaction, organizational commitment, compensation, and career success. Organizations should ensure that mentors provide support and

guidance to mentees to improve their job satisfaction and commitment to the organization[2].

- Formal mentoring programs developed in workplace settings, youth programming, and academic environments across many disciplines can confer the advantages of informal mentoring relationships more systematically and broadly to those who might not otherwise have access to them. Organizations should establish formal mentoring programs to provide access to mentoring for all employees[3].

- Peer mentoring, virtual mentoring, group mentoring, and reverse mentoring are types of mentoring relationships that can benefit employees. Organizations should consider these types of mentoring relationships to provide employees with access to mentoring[4].

- Positive mentee-mentor relationships are vital for maintaining work-life balance and success in careers. Early-career researchers (ECRs) should seek out mentors who can provide support and guidance to improve their work-life balance and career success[5].

- Peer mentoring is perceived among trainees as enhancing their profession-wide competencies during their training. Organizations should establish peer mentoring programs to provide trainees with access to mentoring that can improve their professional competencies[6].

- Mentors should provide a holding environment that supports the identity work of their mentees. Organizations should train mentors to provide a holding environment that supports the identity work of their mentees to improve their career success[4].

References

1. https://www.ncbi.nlm.nih.gov/pmc/articles/PMC2352144/

2. https://www.ncbi.nlm.nih.gov/pmc/articles/PMC 2855142/
3. https://www.ncbi.nlm.nih.gov/books/NBK552775/
4. https://www.ncbi.nlm.nih.gov/pmc/articles/PMC 8124863/
5. https://www.ncbi.nlm.nih.gov/pmc/articles/PMC 8490489/
6. https://www.ncbi.nlm.nih.gov/pmc/articles/PMC 8296284/

Resilience: A Strategy for Building Retention and Success

42. Spectrum: Widen Your Talent Pool for Better Results

Imagine a garden blooming with just one type of flower. Would it be as captivating as a garden filled with an array of colors, shapes, and fragrances? Much like a diverse garden, organizations flourish when they are talents from all walks of life. Are you ready to unearth the gems of diversity, not just as a moral imperative, but also as a strategic tool for increasing your talent pool and boosting employee retention?

Your talent pool should be like a prism, breaking the singular beam of 'conventional hires' into a spectrum of vibrant opportunities. It reflects a multitude of colors— genders, ethnicities, abilities, ages, and orientations—each contributing to the beauty of the spectrum.

Melissa, a Latina software developer, joined a tech startup brimming with diversity but lacking in community spirit. The job was ideal, yet the absence of a unified culture caused her to rethink her career path. What might have happened if her company had skillfully combined diversity with a sense of community?

Priya, an HR manager in a tech firm, was passionate about diversifying her company's predominantly male engineering team. She collaborated with women's coding boot camps and minority-centered tech organizations to recruit a wider range of candidates. Within a year, not only had the engineering team become more diverse, but the company also witnessed a surge in innovative solutions and a more harmonious work culture.

Expanding your talent pool to include all types of diversity isn't just a box to be checked. It's a testament to the kind of organization you are building—one that values human dignity and unique talents.

As you read the list, ask yourself which of these you may have unconsciously excluded from your workplace.

1. **Age Diversity:** Different age groups, from baby boomers and Gen X to millennials and Gen Z, bring varied experiences and perspectives.
2. **Cognitive Diversity:** Refers to differences in how people think, perceive, and approach problems.
3. **Educational Diversity:** Workers with different levels of education, disciplines of study, and areas of expertise.
4. **Parental Status:** Being a parent, especially of young children or children with special needs, can bring a different perspective.
5. **Marital Status:** Single, married, divorced, or widowed employees might have different life experiences.
6. **Socioeconomic Diversity:** Workers from different socioeconomic backgrounds, which can influence perspectives and experiences.
7. **Physical Appearance:** Differences in height, weight, hairstyle, tattoos, piercings, etc.
8. **Lifestyle & Hobbies:** People might be part of certain subcultures or have hobbies that significantly influence their identity.
9. **Socio-Political Views:** Employees may have different political beliefs, affiliations, or levels of activism.
10. **Work Style:** Different approaches to tasks, teamwork, and problem-solving.
11. **Personality Types:** Diversity in temperament, such as introverts versus extroverts.
12. **Health Status:** This can encompass chronic illnesses or conditions.
13. **Ethnic/Racial Diversity:** Differences based on ethnicity and race.
14. **Gender Diversity:** Including men, women, and non-binary or genderqueer individuals.

15. **Sexual Orientation:** This includes lesbian, gay, bisexual, asexual, pansexual, and other non-heterosexual orientations.
16. **Cultural Diversity:** Arising from different nationalities, languages, customs, and traditions.
17. **Religious Diversity:** Employees may belong to various religions, hold different beliefs, or have no religious beliefs at all.
18. **Disability & Physical Abilities:** This includes employees with physical, mental, or emotional disabilities or challenges.
19. **Neurodiversity:** Recognizing differences in brain function, such as individuals on the autism spectrum, those with ADHD, dyslexia, etc.
20. **Skills & Experience:** Diversity in skills, professional backgrounds, and work experience.
21. **Veteran Status:** Those who have served in the military might have unique experiences and perspectives.
22. **Language Diversity:** Workers who speak different languages or have varied language proficiencies.
23. **Geographic Diversity:** Refers to where individuals are from, which can be as broad as international differences or as localized as regional differences within the same country.
24. **Sensory Diversity:** Differences in how people use their senses, like those who are deaf or blind.
25. **Value & Belief Systems:** Everyone has a unique set of morals, values, and ethics.

I bet you didn't think there were 25 types of diversity before this list!

Isn't the ultimate dream of any organization to create a work environment where everyone—not just a select few—can thrive?

By committing to diversity and inclusion, we're not merely following a trend. We are listening to the collective yearning for equal opportunity and fulfilling careers, irrespective of one's background.

Sometimes we exclude people from our work cultures because of unconscious biases. Saying something like, "Well, this kind of work is tough for this kind of person," may just be a sign of not thinking more flexibly about the job.

For example, when I do keynotes about sales, I like to emphasize that not every salesperson needs to be able to do every skill. Many companies have codified this kind of thinking into their process, but some haven't. The idea is that:

- **Hunting & Networking:** At the beginning, you have to find and attract new prospective buyers. Some people have marketing or "hunting" skills and love doing this kind of work, but don't really like talking to the prospects. Other people love the relationship part of sales, and don't like to spend time looking for new people.
- **Qualifying:** When you first talk to the prospect, you may need to screen them to see if they're a good fit for your services, or which products are the best for them. This is a rather mechanical and logical process. Not every salesperson is good at it- particularly if they focus a lot on the relationship.
- **Rapport:** In some selling situations, you need to build a lot of rapport with the prospect. For big or long-term purchases, trust and culture-fit may be a big deal. So, you need a real people-person who loves building relationships with new people.
- **Closing:** When it comes to closing the deal, getting the agreement, and getting the contract signed, some people are good at that, but not rapport- and some people that are good at rapport aren't good at closing.

Sure, sometimes you have a person who is good at all four of those phases above, but they are rare. So, if your company is set up to require everyone to do all four things, you're going to have problems. Once we start seeing that everyone needs a different seat on the bus, you can not only include more people, but you can build a stronger team where each person is an all-star at their part of the job.

The goal is to create a self-sustaining ecosystem where diversity begets innovation, which in turn fosters greater employee retention and attracts even more diverse talent.

So, if you want to start including more types of people to bring new strengths to your organization, here are some ways to do that:

- **Broaden Job Descriptions:** Sometimes, job descriptions can be restrictive, favoring only those with certain degrees or backgrounds. Consider what skills are genuinely necessary for the role and avoid being overly prescriptive.
- **Unconscious Bias Training:** All staff, especially those in hiring positions, should be trained to recognize and combat their unconscious biases, ensuring fairer hiring decisions.
- **Flexible Work Arrangements:** Offer arrangements like remote work, part-time positions, flexible hours, and job sharing, which can be particularly attractive to candidates with varied needs and life circumstances.
- **Inclusive Benefits:** Offer benefits that cater to diverse needs, such as parental leave for both parents, coverage for mental health services, or faith-based holidays.
- **Internship and Apprenticeship Programs:** Engage younger talent or those looking for a career change through structured training programs, allowing them to gain the necessary experience and skills.

- **Hire for Potential:** Instead of exclusively focusing on experience, consider hiring for potential and a willingness to learn.
- **Seek Diverse Hiring Channels:** Beyond traditional job boards, tap into organizations, groups, or platforms that cater to diverse professionals.
- **Create Employee Resource Groups (ERGs):** ERGs can offer support, mentorship, and advocacy for employees from diverse backgrounds.
- **Mentorship and Sponsorship Programs:** Develop programs that connect younger or less experienced employees with seasoned professionals, ensuring that underrepresented groups have opportunities for advancement.
- **Accessible Workplaces:** Ensure that physical and digital spaces are accessible to all, including those with disabilities.
- **Inclusive Culture:** Foster a workplace culture where everyone feels they belong and are valued. This can be cultivated through training, team-building exercises, and open communication channels.
- **Regular Feedback Mechanisms:** Implement regular surveys and feedback channels to understand employees' needs and concerns, ensuring they are continuously met.
- **Transparent Progress Metrics:** Measure diversity and inclusion metrics and share them transparently with the organization. This keeps everyone accountable and highlights areas that need improvement.
- **Global Mindset:** With the increasing feasibility of remote work, consider sourcing talent from around the world, thereby increasing diversity and accessing talent that may not be available locally.
- **Tailored Recruitment Marketing:** Create marketing campaigns that speak to different groups,

showcasing the company's inclusive culture and values.

- **Active Community Engagement:** Engage in community projects and sponsor events that resonate with diverse populations, showing genuine investment in a broader community.

Some may argue that focusing on diversity could detract from merit. On the contrary, diversity and merit are not mutually exclusive; they complement each other. A diverse team brings a plethora of viewpoints, elevating the quality of work and decision-making.

Real-world example: Take Salesforce, a company that has set the gold standard for championing diversity. Their commitment is evident in their hiring practices, employee resource groups, and a pay audit to address gender wage gaps—all contributing to high retention rates.

Imagine your organization has an ongoing partnership with educational institutions serving underprivileged communities. Students from these institutions are given internship opportunities, and the standout performers are offered jobs. This not only broadens the talent pool but also instills a strong sense of loyalty among these employees, knowing that they are valued for their skills and not just their backgrounds.

Diversity is more than a buzzword or a quota. It's a robust strategy for widening your talent pool and amplifying employee retention. By assembling diverse talents, we can create a masterpiece of innovation, loyalty, and shared success.

Ready to transform your organization into a kaleidoscope of talents and opportunities?

The Research

Findings and recommendations on how diversity of employees improves employee retention:

- Creating a sense of community among workers can improve employee retention[1].

- Workforce diversity can help to increase organizational competitive advantages and retain diverse talents[2].
- Diversity beliefs and leadership expertise can moderate and mediate the impact of diversity on organizational performance[3].
- Valuing diversity and inclusion in the workforce can motivate organizations to develop long-term career plans to retain talent[4].
- Valuing intersectionality in the training, development, retention, and design of scientific teams can enrich the work of research[5].
- Developing programs to broaden diversity amongst qualified applicants can improve diversity and inclusion in the healthcare workforce[6].
- Inclusive HRM and employee learning-oriented behaviors can manage the negative impact of workforce diversity[2].

References

1. Rosales, R., León, I. A., & León-Fuentes, A. L. (2022). Recommendations for Recruitment and Retention of a Diverse Workforce: A Report from the Field. Behavior Analysis in Practice, 1-10.
2. Liu, J., Zhu, Y., Wang, H., & Sorooshian, S. (2023). Managing the negative impact of workforce diversity: The important roles of inclusive HRM and employee learning-oriented behaviors. Frontiers in Psychology, 14, 1117690.
3. Turi, J. A., Khastoori, S., & Sorooshian, S. (2022). Diversity impact on organizational performance: Moderating and mediating role of diversity beliefs and leadership expertise. PloS one, 17(7), e0270813.
4. Rotenstein, L. S., Reede, J. Y., & Jena, A. B. (2022). Addressing workforce diversity-a quality-

improvement framework. New England Journal of Medicine, 386(20), 1901-1903.

5. Valantine, H. A., Collins, F. S., & National Institutes of Health (2019). The science and value of diversity: closing the gaps in our understanding of inclusion and diversity. Washington, DC: National Institutes of Health.

6. Williams, M. T., & Reeves, A. N. (2020). The Importance of Diversity and Inclusion in the Healthcare Workforce. Journal of racial and ethnic health disparities, 7(5), 823-830.

43. Flex: Boost Productivity and Morale Through Work Flexibility

Picture a bustling city street, where cars are caught in a gridlock, horns blaring, and everyone is running late for work. Now, imagine a parallel universe where the roads are free-flowing, and people have the time to sip their coffee and read the morning news. Which scenario would you prefer to be a part of? Flexible work arrangements can be the avenue to this utopian work-life harmony.

In a world where work never stops, the 9-to-5 grind can be as dated as a pager in an iPhone era. Let's delve into the transformative power of work flexibility. What if you could own your time, reduce stress, and even improve your health—all while being more productive at your job?

Are you tied to your desk, or do you command your workspace? Flexible work arrangements unshackle employees from rigid time constraints. The freedom to choose when to start and finish work fosters a sense of control that can lead to increased job satisfaction. Furthermore, it creates a culture where people are evaluated based on the quality of their work, not the hours they put in.

Three Benefits You Can't Ignore

- Greater work-to-home enrichment
- Enhanced work-life balance
- Increased job autonomy

What's the point of offering such freedom? It's about mutual trust and respect between employers and employees, cultivating an ethical environment that appreciates individuality and promotes mental well-being.

Have you ever felt like you're burning the candle at both ends? Long hours, time pressures, and lack of control can leave employees fatigued and stressed. By permitting flextime or compressed workweeks, employers are giving a valuable gift—the gift of health. When people have the time to balance work with personal responsibilities, there is a direct, positive impact on their overall well-being.

Flexibility is not the enemy of productivity; it's the catalyst. When people are allowed to work in a manner that aligns with their life commitments and biological clocks, they don't just work more efficiently—they work smarter. Employees who are given the opportunity to utilize flexible work arrangements show enhanced problem-solving abilities and innovation.

Let's Get Real

- Flexibility empowers employees.
- Flexibility enriches lives.
- Flexibility elevates businesses.

Is your organization ready to take the leap into the future?

If so, you're probably wondering, "How can I bring these changes into my own workplace?" Here's your road map:

Five Steps to a More Flexible Future

1. Evaluate current work practices and identify room for flexibility.
2. Establish a clear flexible work policy.
3. Train managers to support flexible work environments.
4. Pilot the flexibility program with a small team.
5. Measure the results and adjust the program accordingly.

If you could visit your workplace five years from now, how would it look? Imagine less turnover, increased morale, and sky-high productivity. Flexible work arrangements are more than a retention strategy; they're a catalyst for transformative business practices.

Embracing work flexibility is like opening a treasure chest of benefits, from increased job satisfaction and reduced turnover to improved health and productivity. Don't you want to be part of a workforce that's not just surviving but thriving? Make the change. The future is flexible, and it's yours to shape.

The Research

Findings and recommendations on how work flexibility improves employee retention based on research:

- Flexible work arrangements such as flexible working hours, compressed workweek, and working from home can help employees experience greater work-to-home enrichment, leading to higher job satisfaction and lower turnover intentions[3].
- Offering flexible work options can have a positive impact on employees' health, work-life balance, and job happiness[4].
- Flexible work arrangements provide employees with more job autonomy in work practices, which enhances their feelings of control over their work and reduces turnover[5].
- Greater employee flexibility can promote retention, especially for employees with chronic overloads and time strains[6].
- Flextime, which involves a variable work schedule, allows workers to choose their own start and finish times, leading to increased job satisfaction and reduced turnover intentions[2].
- Providing employees with the opportunity to use flexible work arrangements can increase their productivity and efficiency when solving business tasks, which benefits both the employee and the employer[3].
- Flexible work arrangements can positively impact employee engagement, which in turn reduces turnover intentions[3].

References

1. Azar, S., Shahtalebi, B., & Gholipour, A. (2021). The relationship between work-to-home enrichment and turnover intention: the mediating role of job satisfaction. Journal of Management Development, 40(3), 258-270.
2. Biron, M., & van Veldhoven, M. (2020). Flexibility at work: It is more than we thought. International Journal of Environmental Research and Public Health, 17(5), 1673.
3. Tsen, M. K., Gu, M., Tan, C. M., & Goh, S. K. (2021). The effect of flexible work arrangements on turnover intention: Does job independence matter?. International Journal of Sociology, 51(2), 141-157.
4. Kim, J. H., & Lee, J. H. (2023). The moderating effect of flexible work option on structural empowerment and generation Z contextual performance. Sustainability, 15(6), 3054.
5. Lott, Y. (2020). More flexible and more innovative: the impact of flexible work arrangements on the innovation behavior of knowledge employees. Journal of Business Research, 113, 1-10.
6. Armstrong, C., Flood, P. C., Guthrie, J. P., Liu, W., MacCurtain, S., & Mkamwa, T. (2010). The impact of diversity and equality management on firm performance: Beyond high performance work systems. The International Journal of Human Resource Management, 21(8), 1176-1193.

44. Cohesion: Cross-Generational Strategies for a Stronger Workforce

Do you recall the age-old proverb, "It takes a village to raise a child"? In a similar vein, it takes a multigenerational workforce to raise an organization to its pinnacle of success. The question, however, is how can we tap into the wisdom and innovation across generations to improve teamwork, productivity, and ultimately, retention? This chapter unravels the secret recipe for a reciprocal learning environment that benefits everyone, regardless of age.

Consider your organization as a loom, weaving together threads of varied colors and textures—each representing a different generation. Some threads are strong, some are vibrant, and some are incredibly intricate. When woven together, they create a fabric stronger and more beautiful than any single thread could achieve alone.

Take the case of Nancy, a Baby Boomer with excellent managerial skills, and Ahmed, a Millennial with a knack for digital marketing. At first glance, they seemed worlds apart. However, when they collaborated on revamping a project, their skills meshed perfectly. Ahmed introduced Nancy to data analytics, while Nancy coached Ahmed in the art of effective communication. Together, they presented a project so well-rounded that it became a template for future ventures.

What Each Generation Brings to the Table

- **Silent Generation:** Institutional Knowledge and Professional Ethics
- **Baby Boomers:** Management Skills and Emotional Intelligence
- **Gen X:** Adaptability and Analytical Thinking
- **Millennials:** Technological Proficiency and Creative Problem-Solving
- **Gen Z:** Digital Natives with a Focus on Individuality

Every generation has a trove of expertise and experiences to share. It is our ethical responsibility to create platforms where such knowledge transfer is not only encouraged but celebrated.

What's the bedrock of any successful relationship, be it personal or professional? Isn't it mutual respect and the willingness to learn from each other?

We all yearn for validation and the opportunity to share our skills and wisdom. By setting up a culture of intergenerational knowledge-sharing, we answer this collective call for reciprocal growth and acknowledgment.

Imagine a workplace where regular "knowledge exchange" forums are held, each time hosted by a different generation. The potential for increased productivity, teamwork, and retention in such an environment is not just significant—it's monumental.

While some might see a multigenerational workforce as a ground for potential conflict, we see it as an unparalleled opportunity. The seemingly contrasting strengths of each generation can actually be the missing pieces to each other's puzzles.

Real-world example: Johnson & Johnson has a well-established program that encourages employees to seek mentors from different generations. This program has not only resulted in improved cross-generational relationships but has also led to higher retention rates.

Let's picture an organization where an internal app is developed solely for the purpose of intergenerational skill sharing. You log in and find a list of quick, five-minute videos—ranging from "The Art of Networking" by a seasoned Baby Boomer to "Basics of Python Coding" by a Gen Z whiz kid. Such an initiative would turbo-charge both productivity and a sense of community.

Here are some strategies for facilitating intergenerational learning:

- **Mentoring Programs:** Pair younger employees with more seasoned professionals. This can allow younger workers to gain from the experience and wisdom of older workers, while older workers can get insights into new technology and changing societal norms.

- **Reverse Mentoring:** This is where younger employees mentor older employees. It's especially useful for staying up to date with technological advancements, social media, or emerging market trends that younger generations may be more familiar with.
- **Workshops and Training Sessions:** Organize sessions where each generation can share their strengths. For example, a Baby Boomer might lead a workshop on effective communication skills, while a Gen Z employee might lead a session on leveraging social media for business.
- **Team Projects:** Create diverse teams in terms of age and encourage collaborative projects. This can naturally foster the sharing of different perspectives and insights.
- **Open Discussions and Forums:** Organize open discussion sessions where employees can share experiences and challenges related to their generation. This can facilitate empathy and understanding.
- **Storytelling Sessions:** Encourage employees from different generations to share their personal stories, challenges, and successes. This can humanize each generation and break down stereotypes.
- **Resource Groups:** Create groups for different generations to meet and discuss common challenges and opportunities. This can also be an avenue for the group to voice concerns or make suggestions to management.
- **Feedback Systems:** Ensure there are robust feedback systems in place. Older employees might be more comfortable with traditional feedback

mechanisms, while younger employees might prefer digital platforms.

- **Lunch and Learn Sessions:** These are casual meetings where employees can eat together and learn something new. Invite speakers from different generations.
- **Job Rotation/Shadows:** Allow employees to spend a day or a week shadowing a colleague from a different generation. This can provide firsthand experience of the skills and strengths of another generation.
- **Celebrate Generational Milestones:** Acknowledge significant generational events or milestones, such as the anniversary of a major world event that heavily impacted a particular generation.
- **Continuous Learning:** Encourage continuous learning and provide resources for employees of all ages to develop new skills.
- **Promote Inclusivity:** It's important for leaders to model inclusive behaviors and promote a culture where all voices are heard and valued.
- **Challenge Stereotypes:** Stereotypes can be barriers to understanding and collaboration. Create awareness programs that challenge generational myths.
- **Leverage Technology:** Use collaborative tools and platforms that cater to various tech comfort levels. This could include anything from traditional email and phone calls to newer collaboration tools like Slack or Teams.

Leadership should be proactive in emphasizing the value of each generation, promoting the idea that every age group brings something valuable to the table. By creating a culture of respect, curiosity, and continuous learning, businesses can leverage the strengths of every generation to their advantage.

Intergenerational learning is not a one-way street where the young learn from the old or vice versa. It's a bustling intersection where knowledge and skills are freely exchanged, enhancing teamwork and productivity while supercharging retention rates. After all, when everyone is both a teacher and a student, the potential for growth is boundless.

Are you ready to turn your workplace into a dynamic classroom where everyone learns from each other?

45. Feedback: Customize Feedback Strategies for Multigenerational Teams

We all yearn for feedback, that vital ingredient that shapes our performance and nurtures our growth. Yet, in a workplace buzzing with Baby Boomers to Gen Z, one size doesn't fit all. So, what's the secret sauce to ensuring that your feedback mechanism isn't just a monotonous echo but a dynamic conversation across generational divides? Imagine a workspace where feedback flows as naturally as water, nourishing every seed—no matter when it was planted.

Feedback is the perfume of relationships at work. One whiff can either draw people closer or repel them. Imagine you're smelling lavender; its comforting scent makes you feel relaxed and at ease. That's what well-executed feedback should be like, especially when you're dealing with a collection of age groups. Each generation has its unique scent preferences, and recognizing those can transform your feedback from a generic spray to a personalized aroma that lingers positively.

Remember Sarah, the Baby Boomer who found emailed feedback too impersonal, or Tim, the Millennial, who wanted Slack updates instead of long meetings? These are not mere quirks but generational preferences. When Sarah was given a face-to-face commendation, her performance soared. And guess what? Tim started hitting all his targets once his manager started sending concise Slack messages. These emotional anchors remind us that adapting our feedback style is not pandering; it's effective communication.

So, how fluent are you in the language of feedback across generations? Can you tell when a long, detailed review is valued or when it could become an overwhelming read? Question your current feedback strategies—are they flexible enough to meet the different needs of each generation?

Look at feedback through a prism. You'll find it refracts into different shades—formal, casual, immediate, or reflective. Just as a prism refracts light into various colors, your feedback should adapt to illuminate the different generational preferences at your organization. For example, while a Gen Xer might prefer feedback with a detailed action plan, a Gen Z might find a quick video explanation more relatable.

Key Takeaways

- **Recognize Individual Preferences:** Not all Baby Boomers prefer face-to-face feedback.
- **Be Flexible:** Allow your feedback mechanisms to adapt.
- **Use Multiple Channels:** Employ emails, meetings, and instant messaging smartly.
- **Don't Stereotype:** Generational norms are guidelines, not rules.
- **Make it a Two-Way Street:** Invite feedback about the feedback.

Let's not forget the moral imperative behind a customized feedback strategy. Ethically, it fosters an inclusive environment where each individual, regardless of their generational background, feels heard and valued. And when people feel valued, they're more likely to invest emotionally and intellectually in their roles, thereby reducing turnover.

You don't have to mimic jargon or slang, but understanding the emotional undertones that each generation responds to can make your feedback resonate deeply. The sentiments of respect for elders that might appeal to a Baby Boomer could differ from the Gen Z drive for rapid personal growth.

Trust in your feedback system, and make sure others do too. Phrases like "proven strategies," "evidence-based," or "pioneering approaches" can root your process in a bedrock of credibility, assuring team members that this is more than a managerial whim—it's a robust strategy for success.

Action Steps to Revolutionize Feedback

1. Conduct a generational survey to understand preferences.
2. Update your feedback guidelines to include multi-generational approaches.
3. Train your managers on how to customize their feedback.
4. Implement a pilot program.
5. Measure the effectiveness and iterate.

Imagine a future where every team member, regardless of age, eagerly anticipates feedback because they know it's tailored just for them. Think about a decrease in turnover rates and an uptick in job satisfaction. If you make these hypotheticals a reality, what could your team achieve?

It's time to break the cycle of one-size-fits-all feedback and weave in the rich threads of generational diversity. Recognize, adapt, and implement. The stage is set, the aroma of trust is in the air, and the spotlight is on you. Are you ready to make the leap and revolutionize your feedback loop?

The Research

Here are five findings with recommendations about how each generation prefers feedback at work:

- Feedback should be future-focused and enable and motivate the feedback recipient to improve[1].
- Generational membership is not significantly associated with preferred feedback patterns[2].
- Feedback should be specific and provide a comparison between a trainee's observed performance and a standard[3].
- Millennial and Generation Z employees are demanding a good work environment with factors related to the promotion of a suitable work-life balance, specifically work flexibility[4].

- Teachers' perceptions of effective feedback may not be shared by learners, and teachers are largely unaware of this[5].

References

1. Kluger, A. N., & DeNisi, A. (2020). The future of feedback: Motivating performance improvement through future-focused feedback. Journal of Applied Psychology, 105(6), 641–657.
2. Kogan, J. R., & Shea, J. A. (2023). Preferred Feedback Styles Among Different Groups in an Academic Medical Center. Journal of Graduate Medical Education, 15(2), 173–177.
3. Archer, J. C. (2010). State of the science in health professional education: Effective feedback. Medical Education, 44(1), 1016–1023.
4. Arora, N., Dhole, V., & Generation, Y. (2019). Perspective, engagement, expectations, preferences and satisfactions from workplace; a study conducted in Indian context. Benchmarking: An International Journal, 26(5), 1378–1404.
5. Hattie, J., & Timperley, H. (2007). The Power of Feedback. Review of Educational Research, 77(1), 81–112.

46. Rewards: Tailor Compensation and Benefits to Attract and Retain Talent

Think about financial wellness as a vibrant painting; colorful, layered, and inviting different interpretations from various onlookers. In an era where job hoppers and gig workers are the norm, and five generations work shoulder to shoulder, the financial wellness must be diverse. But can you paint a masterpiece that captures everyone's eyes and makes them want to stay in the gallery?

Remember the first time you held a crisp dollar bill? The texture under your fingers, the smell of freshly minted money? That sensation is universal but experienced differently by each generation. When designing a compensation plan, it must be tactile enough for every age group to grasp its benefits, like that new bill everyone wants to hold onto.

Jill, a Boomer, enjoyed the certainty of her 401(k) and pension plan, while Mike, a Gen Z, wished his employer accepted crypto contributions for retirement plans. These are not mere anecdotes, but the fabric of today's diversified financial priorities. Jill felt secure with traditional options, while the adoption of new-age investments energized Mike. Their emotional experiences with compensation reveal that the old and new can and should coexist.

When was the last time you updated your compensation and benefits plans? Are you still offering the same old pension plans and medical coverage without considering newer, more appealing options? If your answer is a reluctant "yes," it might be time to diversify.

Think about compensation as an equation where one side is weighted with traditional benefits like pensions and healthcare, and the other with trendy perks like remote work allowances and wellness packages. Striking the perfect balance keeps the equation stable, ensuring nobody feels left out.

Core Principles

- **Balance Traditional and Modern:** From pension plans to crypto investment options.

- **Employee Input:** Include all generations in decision-making processes.
- **Versatility:** Provide a menu of benefits for individual choice.
- **Regular Updates:** Keep your offerings fresh and relevant.
- **Transparency:** Clear communication about all benefits and changes.

Creating an inclusive compensation plan isn't just good for business; it's ethically responsible. It fosters diversity and ensures that no one feels left behind based on their generational preferences. Ethically sound plans don't just retain talent; they attract it.

It's not just about the numbers; it's about feeling valued. Use words like "secure your future," "innovative perks," or "customizable plans" to mirror the different emotional wavelengths of your multi-generational workforce.

Confidence can be instilled through phrases like "financially sound," "employee-tested," and "long-term stability." This assures employees of different ages that the company's plans are robust, tried, and proven effective.

Actions to Remaster Your Masterpiece

- Conduct a multi-generational survey on financial wellness.
- Craft a new, diversified compensation and benefits blueprint.
- Test the new offerings in select departments.
- Gather feedback and make necessary adjustments.
- Roll out the comprehensive package company-wide.

Imagine a company where no one leaves due to dissatisfaction with compensation. Picture a workplace where new talent chooses you for your progressive and inclusive financial wellness plans. Can you turn these visions into reality?

Your company's financial wellness offerings are your signature on the masterpiece that is your workplace culture. A well-crafted, ethically balanced, and widely appealing compensation plan is the mark of a master artist in the world of employee retention. So, will your signature be a scribble or a lasting imprint that stands the test of time?

47. Blueprint: A Final Word on Employee Retention Strategies for Every Generation

As we stand at the edge of a new age in workforce management, the horizon ahead looks promising. Yet, those promises will only materialize if we build bridges—bridges between different generations, aspirations, and values. In a workforce more diverse than ever, how do you construct a blueprint for the future that ensures no one is left behind?

Imagine a symphony—each instrument with its own sound yet contributing to a harmonious melody. In the same vein, retention strategies should resound through every level of your organization, creating a symphony that all generations would want to be a part of. When everyone plays their part, the music doesn't just sound good; it feels transcendent.

Take the example of Nora, a Gen Xer who found a new lease on life with flexible work hours, and Sam, a Gen Z newcomer who felt included thanks to your company's mentorship program. Then there's David, a talented Baby Boomer who left because he felt the company's tech focus alienated him. These stories serve as both reminders and lessons that while we've made strides, there is still more ground to cover.

Do you think you've addressed every aspect of employee retention? Are your strategies up-to-date and all-encompassing? These questions aren't to undermine your efforts, but to encourage continual introspection. Are there hidden corners still in need of illumination?

Your retention strategy should be like a well-painted picture where each brushstroke—be it compensation, feedback, or work-life balance—adds strength and beauty. One loose thread, and the whole fabric may unravel. Be attentive to every detail, from traditional benefits to cutting-edge wellness programs.

Final Reminders

- **Continual Learning:** Keep up with generational trends.

- **Open Dialogue:** Foster environments where everyone feels heard.
- **Tailored Approaches:** One size never fits all.
- **Reassess and Iterate:** Complacency is the enemy of innovation.
- **Empower Leadership:** Equip managers to be retention champions.

As we move forward, the beacon guiding us should be one of ethical integrity. A retention strategy that is fair, just, and inclusive isn't a utopian ideal; it's an attainable goal. Striving for this is not only beneficial for your workforce but also sets a standard in the industry.

Language is more than words; it's the embodiment of your corporate culture. Phrases like "your growth is our priority" or "we value your unique contributions" can serve as soulful echoes across the corridors of your organization, resonating with employees young and old alike.

Confidence in your strategy isn't just for your benefit. Phrases like "time-tested solutions," "best-in-class benefits," or "future-proof policies" reinforce the notion that employees are in capable hands, providing a pillar of assurance for every generation.

Action Plan for the Road Ahead

1. Conduct an annual company-wide retention audit.
2. Engage in cross-generational focus groups.
3. Revise and refresh policies based on findings.
4. Implement changes incrementally, monitoring impact.
5. Celebrate successes and address failures transparently.

What if your organization becomes the gold standard for employee retention? Imagine a future where turnover is an archaic concept, replaced by long-term growth. These aren't just pipedreams; you can make them real.

The pages of this book have been a journey, and the insights and strategies discussed are the building blocks for your organization's future. The final blueprint may not yet be fully drawn, but the pencil is in your hands. Are you ready to draft the future, ensuring that every generation finds a home within your organization? Your next step could be a giant leap for your company and a monumental stride for the world of multi-generational employee retention.

If you ever have any questions, feel free to reach out to me through my keynotespeakerbrian.com website.

Best wishes in your business adventure!

-    Brian

Acknowledgements

Writing a book is so much more than the academic and technical effort required- you also need a lot of energy and time. And that is why some of my biggest thanks go to the people who have given me the most emotional support over the last 11 years of keynote speaking and writing.

I also believe that the best solutions to generational discord are based in empathy and on the heart. Those are not favorite topics for many business leaders and are much misunderstood. But caring is essential to harmony, and so those who helped crack open and fill my heart made this book's perspectives and ideas possible.

Most importantly, my wife Lynda and our dogs Sis and Mo are amazing. Unfortunately, Mo passed a few weeks before editing was complete. But as with all our departed beloved, they become our heart's very fiber.

My parents' combination of sincerity and humor, as always, mean the world to me. My sister, Kevin, Indy, and June are a great source of joy.

I would not be who I am without my Grandma Ratliff, who lived to be 105 years old. When I once insisted, "people really *do* laugh at my jokes," she quipped, "People do stupid things!" Her love and humor made a huge impression on me.

Friends now and throughout the years have been my co-explorers, discoverers, and conversation-mates: Jill, Michelle, John and Brandy (and other great people in our neighborhood, brought together by the isolation of pandemic shutdowns), Inna, Nadia, Victor, Stan, Andy, Vince, Barbara, Dave, David, Annika, Don, Steve, Amy, Jessica, Jami, Will, Gerald, Elizabeth, Dee-Ann, Alan, as well as other members (Jamie, Chuck, and David) of our defunct high-school rock band.

Without music and musicians, I would not be the happy Brian I am most of the time, nor would I be even half as productive. A few artists I'd like to mention that made an impact to me while writing The Retention Formula are Hammock, Scar Symmetry, The Beatles, Miracle Tones, Greta Van Fleet, Beck, The National, yes, a little bit of Taylor Swift, Maxwell, Radiohead, the unparalleled M83, Stevie Wonder, The Big Pink, alt-J, Coldplay, Hans Zimmer, School of Seven Bells, Thomas Newman, and Max Richter.

The people of Reddit and the private stories they've shared were indispensable to developing this book. When I first began exploring the Generations topic and looking for insights, I went there to read what Millennials and Gen Z (and occasional Gen X'ers and Boomers) were saying. Here I heard countless specific perspectives and cultivated a gestalt feeling for their private lives and struggles.

It's easy to feel like you're leaving someone out when expressing public gratitude- so I will conclude here by thanking everyone, named or unnamed, who contributed to the book.

Made in the USA
Las Vegas, NV
25 October 2023

79679664R00140